Agricultural Sector Issues in the European Periphery

Productivity, Export and Development Challenges

Edited by

Anastasios Karasavvoglou
Eastern Macedonia and Thrace Institute of Technology
Persefoni Polychronidou
Central Macedonia Institute of Technology

Vernon Series in Economics

VERNON PRESS

www.vernonpress.com

In the Americas:
Vernon Press
1000 N West Street,
Suite 1200, Wilmington,
Delaware 19801
United States

In the rest of the world:
Vernon Press
C/Sancti Espiritu 17,
Malaga, 29006
Spain

Vernon Series in Economics

Library of Congress Control Number: 2017938948

ISBN: 978-1-62273-337-8

Cover design by Vernon Press, using elements selected by freepik.

Table of Contents

INTRODUCTION

The 8th International conference "The Economies of Balkan of Eastern Europe Countries" (EBEEC-2016) which was jointly organized by the Eastern Macedonia and Thrace Institute of Technology, Greece and the University of Split, Croatia in Split, Croatia, May 6-8, 2016 aimed to present research papers related to the wider domain of economic science with the match of events in the wider region of South-Eastern Europe being the point of discussing. This volume includes *the outcome of a collection of papers originally presented at the conference in the primary sector,* chosen according to a peer review process, making significant contributions to their investigation.

The economies of Balkans and Eastern Europe countries have almost completed a course of two decades with significant changes in their characteristics and their adaptation in the new economic environment. Agriculture and the processing, using and trading of agricultural products have an important role in the countries' economies. Primary sector is a vital sector for the economic development and growth of most countries. Several issues of primary sector are discussed in this volume, such as the framework of the common agricultural policy of the European Union, the identification of an opinion leader portrait in agriculture, the characteristics of using ICT tools in the partnerships and internal processes of enterprises throughout the whole agro-food supply chain, the increased need of small-scale artisanal food businesses to seek new markets abroad, the perceptions of Greek olive oil importers in the UK, the barriers that Greek yogurt entrepreneurs face during their export activities, the reasons for the differences in economic performance and the role of capitals or tangible and less tangible factors influencing development outcomes.

The first paper of Marietta Janowicz-Lomott and Krzysztof Łyskawa is entitled "The current situation and developments in the different member states on risk management in agriculture". The authors study the necessity to create a strong, effective and accepted by European farmers' insurance solutions for agriculture under the framework of the Common Agricultural Policy of the European Union.

Tsimitri Paraskevi, Michailidis Anastasios, Partalidou Maria, Belletti Matteo and Loizou Efstratios in the paper entitled "Looking for "the one": Who is the "real" opinion leader in an agricultural cooperative?" intend to answer a critical question: how do we identify an opinion leader portrait in agriculture (specifically in a cooperative). A key point of concern is the profile of these people in terms of the leading features and some other characteristics which will help policy makers and local stakeholders to identify and use them in the agricultural extension work. In order to achieve the above-mentioned aim a field -case study- research was carried out in a typical Greek agricultural cooperative.

János Felföldi, Szilvia Botos, Ádám Péntek, Róbert Szilágyi and László Várallyai in the paper entitled "Studying the ICT management of agri-food sector on supply chain level – the first stage: Analysis of agricultural ICT usage" study the characteristics of using ICT tools in the partnerships and internal processes of enterprises throughout the whole agro-food supply chain.

Liliana Almonte, Tyler Leighton, Sarah Rogers, Pabitra Saikee, Nicola Bulled and Robert Hersh in their paper entitled "Identifying market strategies for Greek specialty products in the United States" study the increased need of small-scale artisanal food businesses to seek new markets abroad. The study used a unique combination of research methods to identify key marketing strategies to direct the actions taken by Greek specialty food producers interested in entering the United States market.

Christos Soulios, Athanasios Bizmpiroulas and Konstantinos Rotsios in the paper entitled "Greek olive oil in the UK: Evidence on the perception of local importers on product characteristics" study the perceptions of Greek olive oil importers in the UK. It examines their perceptions on the characteristics and attributes olive oil consumers in the UK value the most. The findings are presented and analyzed, and their practical implications are discussed.

Zacharias Papanikolaou, Christos Karelakis and Konstadinos Mattas in the paper entitled "An analysis of export barriers perceptions by Greek yogurt exporters" investigate the barriers that Greek yogurt entrepreneurs face during their export activities. Primary data were collected from a survey of 104 Greek yogurt firms through in-depth interviews. The data were analyzed through the application of a series of multivariate methods.

Nataša Tandir and Zafer Konakli in the paper entitled "Exploring the differences in the development of rural areas in Bosnia and Herzegovina" study the reasons for the differences in economic performance and the role of capitals or tangible and less tangible factors influencing development outcomes. Additional aim is to draw lessons from examples of successful communities and to propose measures for policy makers in order to improve socio-economic status of less successful communities.

Chapter 1

THE CURRENT SITUATION AND DEVELOPMENTS IN THE DIFFERENT MEMBER STATES ON RISK MANAGEMENT IN AGRICULTURE

Marietta Janowicz-Lomott[1] and Krzysztof Łyskawa[2]

[1] Warsaw School of Economics, Collegium of Management and Finance, Institute of Banking and Business Insurance, Niepodległości 162, 02-534 Warsaw, mjanow@sgh.waw.pl

[2] Poznan University of Economics, al. Niepodległości 10, 61-875 Poznań, Polska, K.Lyskawa@ue.poznan.pl

ABSTRACT

In the framework of the Common Agricultural Policy provides the ability of using a variety of instruments supporting agriculture in emergency and crisis: subsidies for crop insurance and livestock, conducting mutual fund or to organize a fund stabilization of an income. A great number of Member States decided to use such instruments, but they also showed significant restrictions in daily use. Although these instruments can be funded by the EU, many countries decided to use their own, funded by the country's arrangements for risk management in agriculture. In the next 3-4 years, it is necessary to build a strong, effective and accepted by European farmers insurance solutions for agriculture. If Transatlantic Trade and Investment Partnership (TTIP) sign the farmers, there will be in Europe a lot of poor protection as compared to farmers in the United States in case of a sudden weather phenomena, but also the damage caused by pests or falling price levels. The article is an attempt to indicate the necessary direction of these changes.

KEYWORDS

Risk management, subsidies for crop insurance and livestock, aquiculture insurance, mutual, European Common Agricultural Policy.

JEL CLASSIFICATION CODES

Q18, G22, D81

1. INTRODUCTION

There are no uniform solutions for insurance in the agricultural industry in the EU countries, since every state has its own geographical and climatic specificity and, as a result, the scope and frequency of damages vary. In France, Italy and Spain the agricultural natural disasters results insurance systems have been functioning for more than 40 years, with an active participation of the state. In some countries (like Greece) there have been attempts to introduce compulsory insurance. For many years in Scandinavia there has been a notion of so-called regional solidarity, which means that all purchased policies participate in gathering funds for natural disaster compensations. The objective of this article is to find out what risk management instruments are used in the particular EU countries and what types of insurance can be used in this scope. This paper is based on research conducted among the member states of Copa-Cogeca.

2. THE REASONS FOR INCREASE OF INTEREST IN RISK MANAGEMENT IN AGRICULTURE IN THE EU AGRICULTURAL POLICY

Activity connected to plant production and, indirectly, also to animal husbandry, depends largely on the natural seasons cycle and weather phenomena. There are several industries that – as in the case of agriculture – must consider the influence of weather in the scope of their business (e.g. food industry, heating industry, some types of services), although their impact on the functioning of the economy as a whole is not that significant. The variability of weather and its consequences are the factors that introduce constant uncertainty concerning the assumed amount and quality of crops into the lives of farmers. Losses in cultivation caused by adverse climatic and weather conditions at a given stage of growth cannot be compensated as in normal production processes, like for example in factories by using additional human capital and greater use of machines, and are carried over to further stages of production bringing an inevitable loss of profitability. Even the plant growth itself is closely limited by photosynthesis, which is why the production cycle in agriculture cannot be conducted with such methods as the ones used in other branches of national economy, where production can be conducted in shifts even 24 hours a day.

Table 1. Extreme Events in Europe 1999-2015

December 1999	Winter storms in western and central Europe.
	Heavy precipitation and extremely high wind speed.
August 2002	Heavy precipitation and floods along central European rivers.
	Economic losses exceeded 15 billion EURO
Summer 2003	Heat wave in central and western Europe.
	Extremely high temperatures for weeks led to more than 30.000 deaths and extreme drought across Europe. More than 25.000 fires burnt 650.000 hectares
Summer 2005	Heat and drought in southern Europe.
	Extremely high temperatures. Significantly less precipitation than average
Winter 2006	Extreme cold in eastern and central Europe.
	Minimum temperature was 4-12°C colder than the 1961-1990 mean
Mild winter 2007	Winter of 2007 ranked among the warmest ever recorded in large part of Europe.
	Average temperature anomalies were more than 4°C
May 2008	Flash floods in central Europe
Summer 2008	Floods across eastern Europe river.
	Nearly 50.000 homes were submerged, more than 30.000 hectares of farmland was destroyed.
Winter 2009	The winter of 2009 was colder than usual in central and western Europe
Spring 2010	Flooding in Poland and Eastern Europe. In May 2009, the precipitation amount was 100 mm above the long-term mean across vast regions of eastern Europe. Total flood damage exceeded 2,5 billion Euro
Winter 2010	Unusually cold, snowy winter in Europe. Most areas of Europe saw between 10 and 20 additional ice days than normal from December through February. Due to the prolonged cold temperatures and the frequency of snow storms, the number of days with more than 1 cm of snow on the ground was significantly greater than normal across Europe
February 2010	Severe winter storms in Europe. Tropical storm Xyntia passed through Portugal, Spain, France, Belgium, the Netherlands and Germany, causing heavy rainfall and high wind speed

Summer 2010	Heat and drought in eastern Europe. This region was hit by record temperatures; very low rainfall amounts resulted in crop losses, peat and forest fires. Mean temperature was between 4 and 8°C higher than the long-term average during July and August. For many regions, there were at least 10 and up to 30 more summer days than normal during July 2010
Summer 2011	Widespread drought in Europe
Winter 2013	Extreme rainfall and flooding in Europe
Summer 2014	Extreme rainfall and flooding in Europe affecting Bosnia-Herzegovina
Summer 2015	Drought in Europe "extreme weather belt" linked to worst drought since 2003. Severe droughts that stretched across a central European band this summer are consistent with climate models for a warming continent
Summer 2015	Flooding in southern France caused by heavy rain killed at list 15 people and left 12 missing near France's Mediterranean coast. More than 350 mm of rain fell on the Var department in southern France in a few hours, triggering flooding that surged in some places to two meters over normal levels
Autumn 2015	Heavy rain and flooding Italy (Pisa, Florence), Croatia, Serbia, Bosnia (5-deaths)

Source: (van der Linden et al., 2015)

The key parameters for assessment of production significance of agriculture for the EU economy differ in various member states, however, all of them indicate that this sector is important not only from the perspective of satisfying nutrition needs of the EU citizens, but it is also a significant element of the EU economy.

The share of agriculture in generation of GDP depends on the level of economic development of individual countries. In 2014 for UE-28 it amounted to 1.6%. The largest share of agriculture in GDP was noted in the "young" member states: Romania (5.4%) and Bulgaria (5.3%). (Chart 1).

Chart 1. The share of agriculture in generation of GDP in EU countries

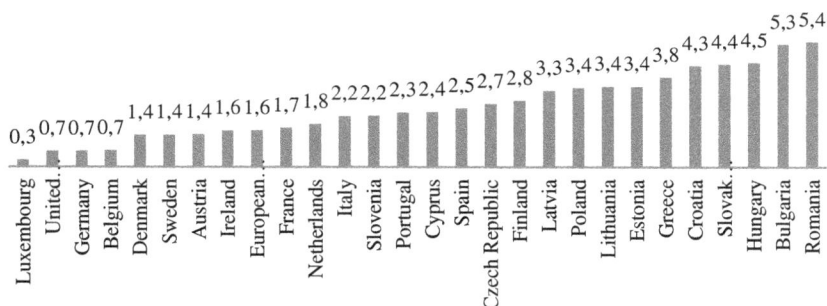

Luxembourg 0,3; United. 0,7; Germany 0,7; Belgium 0,7; Denmark 1,4; Sweden 1,4; Austria 1,4; Ireland 1,6; European. 1,6; France 1,7; Netherlands 1,8; Italy 2,2; Slovenia 2,2; Portugal 2,3; Cyprus 2,4; Spain 2,5; Czech Republic 2,7; Finland 2,8; Latvia 3,3; Poland 3,3; Lithuania 3,4; Estonia 3,4; Greece 3,4; Croatia 3,8; Slovak. 4,3; Hungary 4,4; Bulgaria 4,5; Romania 5,3; 5,4

Source: World Bank

The size of agricultural production in UE-28 in 2014 amounted to 415 691 million EURO and an increase has been noted since 2005 (apart from a decrease in 2009) (Table 2). The largest food manufacturers in EU are France, Italy, Germany, Spain and the United Kingdom. In 2014 Poland was 7th in this ranking.

Table 2. The share of Member States in the EU's agricultural production in 2014

Country	Total production (mln EURO)	Shared of EU - 28 (%)
EU - 28	415 055,00	100
France	73 994,40	17,8
Germany	57 637,00	13,9
Italy	53 793,90	13,0
Spain	42 116,00	10,1
United Kingdom	31 678,50	7,6
Netherlands	27 134,90	6,5
Poland	22 730,50	5,5
Romania	16 770,80	4,0
Denmark	11 009,60	2,7
Greece	10 394,40	2,5
Belgium	8 045,30	1,9

Hungary	7 812,30	1,9
Ireland	7 367,00	1,8
Austria	6 951,20	1,7
Portugal	6 526,50	1,6
Sweden	6 201,40	1,5
Czech Republic	4 936,40	1,2
Bulgaria	4 159,30	1,0
Finland	4 197,60	1,0
Lithuania	2 575,60	0,6
Slovakia	2 385,90	0,6
Croatia	2 008,50	0,5
Latvia	1 216,70	0,3
Slovenia	1 249,50	0,3
Estonia	896,3	0,2
Cyprus	694,2	0,2
Luxembourg	447,9	0,1
Malta	124,1	0,0

Source: own work on the basis of EUROSTAT data http://ec.europa.eu/eurostat/statistics-explained/index.php/Agricultural_accounts_and_prices

The situation on the market of agricultural products has changed significantly in recent years. Nowadays agricultural activity is characterized by greater market orientation. Agriculture is not only a food production it is a business which gives more opportunities, but also vulnerabilities. We can also observe growing role of factors outside agricultural demand and supply - agricultural policy, technological changes, restrictions (Fan, 1991).

Agricultural markets are also characterized by significant price volatility. A certain amount of volatility on the agricultural markets is normal, because agriculture is subject to good and bad years. But at the same time agriculture is a sector in which adaptation to the markets often takes longer, partly because of the characteristics of the production cycle. In the last few years, volatility has increased and has become a constant source of risk for farmers (Chart 2).

Chart 2. Annual food price indices[1]

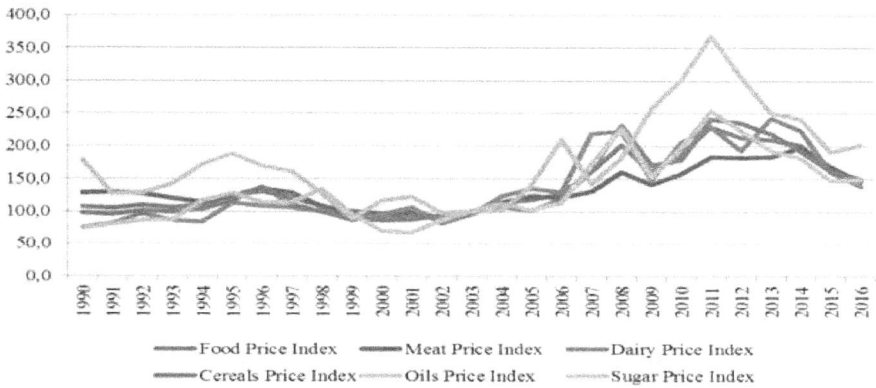

Source: own work on the basis of FAO data

When we looked at in the long term there is little evidence that volatility in international agricultural commodity prices, as measured using standard statistical measures is increasing and this finding applies to both nominal and real prices (Price..., 2011). Volatility has, however, been higher during the decade since 2000 than during the previous decade. Another conclusion that emerges from the study of long-term trends in volatility is that periods of high and volatile prices are often followed by long periods of relatively low and stable prices (OECD-FAO, 2010). Finally, it is well established that agricultural markets are intrinsically subject to greater price variation than other markets. However, as prices become volatile they have a negative impact on the food security of customers, farmers and entire countries (C.L. Glibert&C.W. Morgan 2010).

In the last years, we can also note a large number of extreme climatic events (table 2), connected with climate changes.

3. Financing risk management on agricultural farms from the EU funds

At the EU level, there are various initiatives undertaken that are aimed at mitigating results of events adverse for agriculture. Already in the Resolution of 14 April 2005 on the drought in Portugal the European Commission was called to

---

[1] The FAO Food Price Index is a measure of the monthly change in international prices of a basket of food commodities. It consists of the average of five commodity group price indices, weighted with the average export shares of each of the groups for 2002-2004.See more http://www.fao.org/worldfoodsituation/foodpricesindex/en/

analyse the causes of repeatability of droughts and to check if they are connected to the climatic changes. In other resolutions, the European Parliament is asked to accelerate the introduction of a pilot project concerning EU insurance or compensation system, as well as introduction of changes in the rules of UE solidarity fund in a way that would include help for people suffering from natural disasters. In the Resolution of 18 May 2006 on natural disasters in agriculture the Parliament included arguments pointing to the need for greater financial involvement of the EU in countering and remedying of consequences of natural disasters. In one of the latest documents of 16 April 2013 the European Commission presented a package of activities that included two parts: the EU strategy concerning adaptation to climate change that specifies the scope and mechanisms enabling improvement of the EU readiness for current and future climate change consequences, and the green book connected thereto, which concerns insurance against natural and human-caused disasters. These social consultations open a broad discussion concerning the adequacy and availability of the existing insurance options. They have become a reference point for actions which can be implemented by various sectors (such as agriculture) or by the particular member states in the scope of already permitted activities.

Entities can deal with numerous hazards without a significant external intervention. However, the whole idea of the Common Agricultural Policy is based on a farm functioning stabilisation mechanism [OECD 2011 p. 230].

Chart 3. Division of hazards and ways of coping with their effects in Spain (as an example)

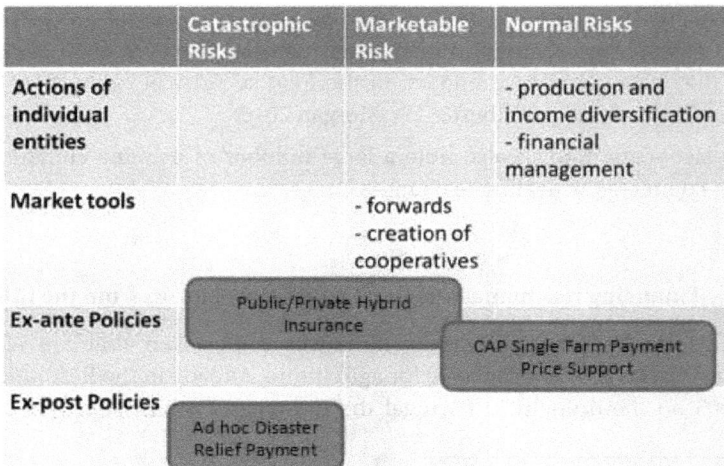

	Catastrophic Risks	Marketable Risk	Normal Risks
Actions of individual entities			- production and income diversification - financial management
Market tools		- forwards - creation of cooperatives	
Ex-ante Policies	Public/Private Hybrid Insurance		CAP Single Farm Payment Price Support
Ex-post Policies	Ad hoc Disaster Relief Payment		

Source: [OECD 2011 p. 231]

Member states undertook numerous actions aimed at financing the effects of fortuitous events in agriculture, however almost every document created in this scope it was noted that making use of the actions allowed by law is possible only in the case of a natural disaster (loss above 30% in a specific farm) that is formally recognised by public authorities. In 2009 (Council Regulation 2009) member states were for the first time allowed to co-finance the insurance premiums paid by the farmers for insurance of their crops, animals and plants and co-financing of compensations for some losses suffered as a result of animal or plant diseases and environmental incidents, in view of the growing significance of effective risk management in agriculture. In reference to crops this may also include losses caused by pests, which provides the opportunity to introduce new products which had not been offered before. It was also established that the contribution to the premium that might be offered by a member state should be about 65% of the due payment. The contribution should be directed at the insurance company operating within the Community and offering the solutions mentioned above. The resolution 73/2009 also introduced a special financial and organizational solution allowing for the payment of compensations to farmers who suffered economic losses as a result of animal or plant diseases and as a result of the so-called environmental incidents. The aim of this solution is to enable the granting of financial contribution in mutual funds.

Mutual fund is a system accredited by a member country according to its national law, which enables affiliated farmers to have joint insurance and owing to which compensation are paid to the farmers affiliated in the fund who suffered economic losses. Therefore, it is a simple instrument (fund), based on the principle of mutuality, though formally speaking it is not an insurance company.[2]

The objective of these actions was to decrease the influence of weather and market phenomena on the functioning of agricultural producers, yet by using the public-private partnership in the form of heavily subsidised and state-regulated insurance. Were it not for these undertakings, those threats would have been considered as non-indemnifiable due to high frequency of their occurrence and lack of reliable information concerning the damages caused [OECD 2011 pp. 230-231].

Another objective of development of subsidised insurance is to limit the help provided after a hazard has taken place. Instead, ex-ante activities have been introduced, their direct financial cost being born not only by the state, but also by the potential victims who pay some part of the insurance premium. The effects could be clearly seen in the case of Spain, where in the period between 2000 and 2005, agricultural producers were paid 22 million euro of ad-hoc aid (after implementation of agricultural production insurance system). Therefore, about

---

[2] This solution was applied in Europe by farmers' associations or agricultural organizations in France, the Netherlands or Italy. See more. (Janowicz-Lomott-Łyskawa, 2013)

3.7 million euro was paid in a year as a result of damages caused by frost, drought and excessive rains. It can be stated that the Spanish government achieved its goal, comparing the 680 million euro that was paid as ad-hoc aid payments in Italy in the period 2001-2006, which gives an average of more than 113 million euro per year [Diaz-Caneja et al. 2009 p. 15]. Disaster support is paid out in Spain if compensation payments are not enough to fulfil the needs arising after the occurrence of disaster hazards.

At the time when the European Union is moving on to another funding period (2014-2020), numerous consultations have been conducted in the scope of ways of financing the effects of fortuitous event in agriculture, which resulted in the preparation of the GREEN PAPER on the insurance of natural and man-made disaster (COM/2013/0213). The main objective was to improve the readiness of Europe in case of natural and man-made disasters, and insurance was to be a special tool in this scope. Michel Barnier, commissioner for internal market and services, stated that natural and man-made disasters are getting more and more frequent, while the ability of the insurance industry to guarantee security in case of such occurrences is not fully utilised. He pointed out that solutions at the European level that would allow to fill this gap on the insurance market need to be found.

Despite the awareness of some drawbacks which concern insurance services (non-indemnifiability of some occurrences, limited financial capacity of the insurer, the possibility of refusal of providing an insurance cover), it is emphasised in literature[3] that it is one of the most effective ways of financing the effects of fortuitous events present in agriculture, commonly used in risk management. When defining the benefits of agricultural producers utilizing insurance, the following should be mentioned in the first place (OECD 2000, p. 108):

- income stabilisation – the compensation paid, especially for losses in crops, allows to stay in the production cycle, without the need to search for additional sources of financing (disaster loan);

- improvement of agricultural producer's credibility when applying for a loan improves his solvency or becomes an additional security;

- the possibility to become involved in new production specialisations, without the consequences of bearing the risk realisation effects individually;

- the certainty of compensations in the scope of concluded agreements (no need to pressure the government *ad hoc* in the face of every individual event).

---

[3]Instead of many: (Hazell et al., 1986, p. 4 and following)

It should be stressed that the governments of individual countries can also benefit from the functioning of an appropriate insurance system in agriculture. The benefits include:

- assurance of stability in functioning of individual entities and, as a result, achievement of objectives stated in *Rural Development Programme*;

- achievement of political or budget objectives (no need to have large reserves for possible *ad hoc* help, financial involvement is known already at the beginning of the budget year);

- complementation of social benefits system resulting in lack of farm abandonment phenomenon or intensive demographical changes in rural areas (intensive ageing of society);

- lesser uncertainty in the functioning of agricultural producers can also limit the inflation pressure in the scope of food prices.

However, the variety of events in the environment, their intensity and most of all the requirements placed before insurance companies in the scope of solvency result in not all incidents being accepted by underwriters. The figure below is an attempt to divide the phenomena concerning agriculture in the assessment of insurance companies. It should be stressed that the same phenomena will be treated in a different way depending on the geographic area. A draught or the effects of poor wintering will not always be treated as unacceptable by the insurance market.

Chart 4. Classification of incidents according to insurance companies from the point of view of their insurability

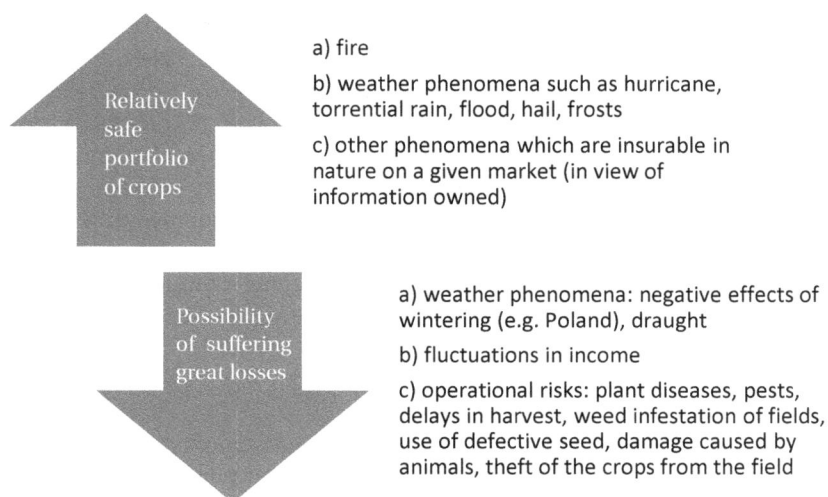

Relatively safe portfolio of crops

a) fire

b) weather phenomena such as hurricane, torrential rain, flood, hail, frosts

c) other phenomena which are insurable in nature on a given market (in view of information owned)

Possibility of suffering great losses

a) weather phenomena: negative effects of wintering (e.g. Poland), draught

b) fluctuations in income

c) operational risks: plant diseases, pests, delays in harvest, weed infestation of fields, use of defective seed, damage caused by animals, theft of the crops from the field

Source: own work

In literature on the subject six characteristics that the insured risk should have are mentioned:

- the insurer as well as the insured should have the same amount of information on the possibility of occurrence of the insured risk;

- there cannot be a positive correlation of the risk of losses between the insured entities;

- the number of insured should be large enough;

- the probability of realization of the risk specified in the policy must be measurable;

- losses suffered by the entities should be clearly defined and easy to estimate;

- possible loss should be significant and the insurance price established at a level accessible for the potential purchaser (Pawłowska-Tyszko et al. 2015, p.118)

As a result of these considerations, the existing risk management tools have been enhanced in the new financial perspective of the Common Agricultural Policy (2014-2020). The first instrument is the subsidy to insurance but with a preferred form of contract execution based on indexes[4]. **Insurance based on an index** is to be understood as a contract in which the amount of the benefit/compensation depends on how the value of a certain determined index (parameter) is shaped, which represents the impact of a given factor on financial results and/or the value of the farmer's crop. If the index is based on weather factors, then the payment from the insurance company is based on how the values of the amount of rainfall, temperature or wind are shaped, and not in reference to the actual crop loss (Łyskawa, Zimowski, 2009, p.286). It is to be emphasised that the adopted calculation method should allow for the reflection of losses suffered individually, by each farmer in a given year. *Mutual funds* are to operate under the current rules, while the scope of mutual funds' operation has been expanded by the effects of harmful organisms and adverse climatic phenomena. Apart from the tools established in 2009 (insurance and mutual funds), there has also appeared an opportunity for a member country to launch an optional tool for the stabilization of agricultural income. Compensation will be paid from the income stabilization fund[5] if the drop in **income exceeds 30%** of the

---

[4] Art. 37 of the Regulation of the European Parliament and of the Council (EU) No 1305/2013 of 17 December 2013 on the support of rural areas development by the European Agricultural Fund for Rural Development (EFRROW) and repealing the Regulation of the Council (EC) No 1698/2005

[5] It must be based on the idea of the mutual fund.

average annual income of an individual farmer[6]. However, the payment cannot compensate for more than 70% of the lost income. It is to be emphasised that the use of the instruments described depends on the decisions of the particular member countries, which may continue co-financing of premiums in agriculture insurance from the national budget or use all or selected instruments co-financed from the CAP means (see chart 5) (Janowicz-Lomott et al. 2014)

Chart 5. Agricultural risk management tools supported from the member countries budget or the EU budget after 2014

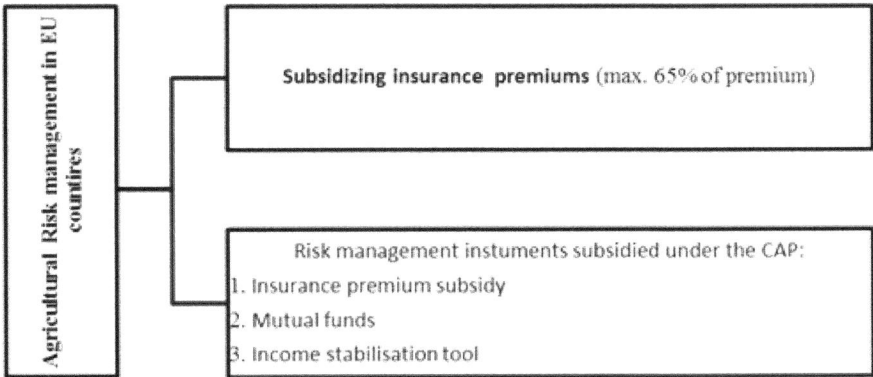

Subsidizing insurance premiums (max. 65% of premium)

Risk management instuments subsidied under the CAP:
1. Insurance premium subsidy
2. Mutual funds
3. Income stabilisation tool

Agricultural Risk management in EU countires

Source: own work.

4. RISK MANAGEMENT POLICY IN THE EU MEMBER COUNTRIES

On the basis of research conducted in the EU member countries it is possible to demonstrate the diversity of instruments applied by them under risk management policy in agriculture (chart 6).

---

[6] Just like in the case of insurance, it is based on the average of three or five years, the best and the worst year excluded.

Chart 6. Types of Risk Management schemes by Member States/Regions

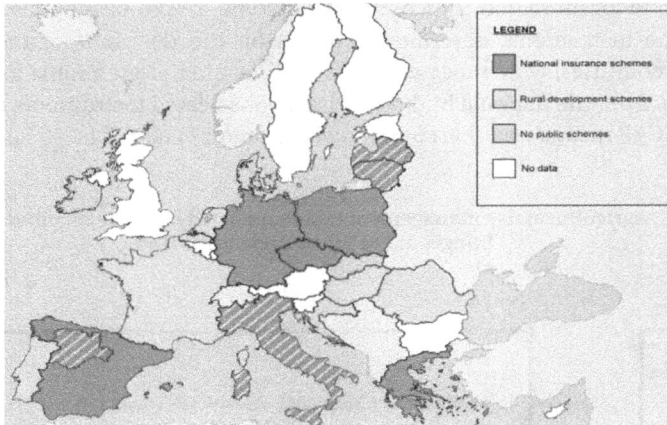

A number of countries is still following the 'old' route which allows to co-finance premiums from the national budget (Table 3)

Table 3. Status of Risk Management at national level

Country	Scope
Austria	Insurance against hail and frost and from 2016 drought
	Support to insurance premium 50% (25% national budget+25% provinces)
Czech Republic	Financed by "Support and Guarantee Agricultural and Forestry Fund" support to insurance premium:
	- 10%-50% crops
	- 25%-50% special crops
Germany	Insurance weather conditions for crops, wine and fruits and vegetables
Italy	Insurance for agricultural structure (nurseries, plants) - livestock
Lithuania	Insurance weather conditions for crops
	Support to insurance premium max.50%
Poland	Insurance costs (65%) Annual establishment of the rate Crops and livestock
Spain	Insurance costs Crops and livestock Removal of dead animals

Source: the own study on the basis of Copa-Cogeca's research

Seven of the member countries utilize agricultural insurance subsidized from the national budget, three of them are new member countries in which the share of agriculture in GDP generation is significantly above the European average.

Varied are both the scope of cover and the scale of the support provided. This method is also used by the greatest manufacturers of food in Europe – Germany (2nd place), Italy (3rd place) and Spain (4th place).

In Germany, the scope of assistance covered only wine and fruits and vegetables, in the case of Italy this system is applied in a limited scope and is also a supplement to the system financed from CAP, in Poland subsidies to insurance relate almost total crop production.

Currently 11 member countries are following the route which allows to gain financing from the EU funds (Table 4). In the majority of cases co-financing of insurance premiums has been applied. Four member countries decided to have the opportunity to create mutual funds, while in the case of the other three member countries it is planned to introduce income stabilization instruments.

Table 4. Status of Rural Development Programme (measure 17, Regulation 1305/2013)

	Insurance	Mutual funds	Income stabilisation tool
Belgium Vlaanderen	Contribution to the cost of insurance (<50%) for weather adverse effects	-	-
Croatia	Costs of insurance <65%	-	-
France National	Costs of insurance	Costs of mutualisation	-
Hungary	Contribution to the cost of insurance for weather adverse effects	-	Income stabilisation for crops
Italy National	Contribution to the cost of insurance for weather adverse effects	Costs of mutualisation	Income stabilisation
Latvia	Costs of insurance for crops	-	-
Lithuania	Costs of insurance (weather and livestock)	-	-
Netherlands	Contribution to the cost of insurance for weather adverse effects	-	-
Portugal Continente	Contribution to the cost of insurance for weather adverse effects	-	-
Portugal Açores	Contribution to the cost of insurance for weather adverse effects	Contribution to the cost of mutualisation for weather adverse effects	-
Portugal Madeira	Contribution to the cost of insurance for weather adverse effects	-	-
Romania	-	Costs of mutualisation	-
Spain Castilla y León	-	-	Income stabilisation tool (milk sector)

Source: the own study on the basis of Copa-Cogeca's research

The means assigned by the member countries to support insurance instruments are shaped in various ways (Table 5).

Table 5. Yearly public expenditure (€) for Risk Management in agriculture

Country	Yearly public expenditure (€)	Country	Yearly public expenditure (€)
Austria	N.A.	Italy	367 257 143
Belgium	734 707	Latvia	1 428 571
Bulgaria	N.A..	Lithuania	2 494 326
Croatia	8 096 196	Luxembourg	0
Cyprus	N.A.	Malta	0
Czech Republic	0	Netherlands	7 714 286
Denmark	0	Poland	50 000 000
Estonia	0	Portugal	7 220 756
Finland	N.A.	Romania	28 571 429
France	85 821 429	Slovakia	0
Germany	N.A.	Slovenia	N.A.
Greece	0	Spain	254 000 000
Hungary	13 616 139	Sweden	N.A.
Ireland	0	United Kingdom	0

Source: the own study on the basis of Copa-Cogeca's research

The biggest expenses are incurred by countries belonging to the group of the greatest agricultural producers (Italy, Spain, France), but among the greatest producers there are also countries (Great Britain) which do not support agricultural risk management instruments financially.

5.   CONCLUSION

The guidelines included in the European Commission's document pointed out to the necessity of using various instruments, including the financial market, so that it is possible to obtain the guarantee of basic income in the case of a crisis situation and in order to keep the liquidity of farms. The Commission points to the fact that this instrument should be available to all farmers who suffered losses as a result of a crisis event, and the amount of payments by way of income stabilisation can be connected with income only and cannot be connected to production type or size of the given producer, prices used locally or abroad in connection to such production or any other production factors.

The aforementioned expectations can be met by basing the financial (insurance) products on the notion of indexes. This would allow both to carry out the Commission's expectations as well as to generate the supply side, that is the insurance companies' offer (at the moment there is no insurance offer for some events in many countries). However, the intent to use the above instrument would require that the member countries establish a precise definition of income and create of a reference income system at the level of farms. Advanced technologies of weather phenomena measurement and registration of events at farms take us closer to the implementation of index insurance mechanism in Europe.

REFERENCES

Council Regulation (EC) No 73/2009 of 19 January 2009 establishing common rules for direct support schemes for farmers under the common agricultural policy and establishing certain support schemes for farmers, amending Regulations (EC) No 1290/2005, (EC) No 247/2006, (EC) No 378/2007 and repealing Regulation (EC) No 1782/2003

Diaz-Caneja M.B,. Conte C. G, Gallego Pinilla F. J., Stroblmair J., Catenaro R., Dittmann C., 2009, Risk Management and Agriculture Insurance Scheme in Europe, European Commission http://ec.europa.eu/dgs/jrc/downloads/jrc_reference_report_2009_09_agri_ins.pdf

Fan S., 1991, Effects of Technological Change and Institutional Reform on Production Growth in Chinese Agriculture, American Journal of Agricultural Economics, vol. 73 (2), pp.266-275, doi: 10.2307/12427

Gilbert C. L. , . Morgan C. W , 2010, Food price volatility, Philosophical Transactions of the Royal Society B, Biological Sciences, volume 365, issue 1554, http://dx.doi.org/10.1098/rstb.2010.0139

Hazell P., Pomareda C., Valdes A., Crop Insurance for Agricultural Development, Johns Hopkins, London 1986,

Janowicz-Lomott, M., & Łyskawa, K. (2014). The new instruments of risk management in agriculture in the European Union. Procedia Economics and Finance, 9, 321-330.

Linden P. van der, Dempsey P., Dunn R., Caesar J., Kurnik B., 2015, Extreme weather and climate in Europe, European Environment Agency, European Topic Centre on Climate Change Impacts, Vulnerability and Adaptation

Łyskawa K., Zimowski M., Ubezpieczenia indeksowe w rolnictwie - wprowadzenie do problematyki, [Index insurance in agriculture – introduction to the subject] w: Inwestycje finansowe i ubezpieczenia - tendencje światowe a polski rynek 2009/60, Uniwersytet Ekonomiczny we Wrocławiu, Wrocław 2009, p.286

OECD, 2000, Income Risk Management in Agriculture, Paris

OECD, 2011, Managing Risk in Agriculture, POLICY ASSESSMENT AND DESIGN, http://www.oecd-ilibrary.org/agriculture-and-food/managing-risk-in-agriculture_9789264116146-en

OECD-FAO, 2010, Agricultural Outlook, OECD/FAO

Pawłowska-Tyszko J., Soliwoda M., Pieńkowska-Kamieniecka S., Walczuk D., 2015, Current status and prospects of development of the tax system and insurance scheme of the Polish agriculture, INSTITUTE OF AGRICULTURAL AND FOOD ECONOMICS NATIONAL RESEARCH INSTITUTE, Warsaw

Price Volatility in Food and Agricultural Markets: Policy Responses, 2011, Policy Report including contributions by European Commission, FAO, IFAD, IMF, OECD, UNCTAD, WFP, the World Bank, the WTO, IFPRI and the UN HLTF

Chapter 2

LOOKING FOR "THE ONE": WHO IS THE "REAL" OPINION LEADER IN AN AGRICULTURAL COOPERATIVE?

Tsimitri Paraskevi[1], Michailidis Anastasios[1], Partalidou Maria[1], Belletti Matteo[2] and Loizou Efstratios[3]

[1]*Aristotle University of Thessaloniki, Greece, Laboratory of Agricultural Extension and Rural Sociology, Department of Agricultural Economics*

[2]*The Polytechnic University of Marche, Italy, Department of Agricultural, Food and Environmental Sciences*

[3]*Technological Educational Institute of Western Macedonia, Greece, Department of Agricultural Technology*
tassosm@auth.gr

ABSTRACT

Farmers today are required to take decisions amidst a constantly changing environment and market condition. They have to work under great uncertainty and risks which make their job even more complex. Towards this direction, it is of high importance to have access to the correct information at the correct time. However, it's not an easy task; how they get their information and who is influencing their decisions, either individual farmers-opinion leaders-or entire networks, formal or informal ones plays an important role. Therefore, if a convergence between leadership self-perception and leadership reputation will be detected, a second interesting issue to develop will be that of outlining a "portrait" of such a leader. This paper tries to answer a critical question: whether people labeled (by others) as opinion leaders in a rural area evaluate themselves as such in other words how do we identify an opinion leader portrait in agriculture (specifically in a cooperative). A key point of concern is the profile of these people in terms of the leading features and some other characteristics which will help policy makers and local stakeholders to identify and use them in the agricultural extension work. In order to achieve the above-mentioned aim a field -case study- research was carried out in a typical Greek agricultural cooperative. Farmers/members of the cooperative were involved in a sample survey in order to determine the degree of their «leadership» (self-evaluated opinion leadership techniques). Then, using a Two-Step Cluster Analysis, the sample was stratified in some discrete clusters depending on the level of «self-evaluated leadership» of each farmer and according to the generalizations of the related theories. Finally, in-depth field research was used to disclose the local leadership network and answer who holds the central positions within this network (recommended opinion leadership). Data were collected through a survey addressing 152 farmers/members of the agricultural cooperative, carried out in April-May 2015. Five different farmers' profiles were identified by self-evaluated leadership characteristics. But only one of these types is actually the "one", that is the real leader who influences other farmers both in terms of self-evaluation and by recommendation. Due to the small sample and due to the limitation of the research to a single cooperative, the study might have generalisability deficiencies. The empirical identification of an opinion leader comprehensive picture is a potentially useful tool both from a descriptive and from a normative optics. Indeed, this picture can be used to improve the organizational learning within an agricultural economy network such as a cooperative, offering significant benefits to the rural society, policy makers and to related economic sectors as a result. The contribution of this research is in having examined, for first time the parameters of opinion leadership in agriculture and rural life for which there has been longstanding interest.

KEYWORDS

Agricultural Cooperative, Farmer, Networking, Opinion Leader, Self-Evaluating Leadership, Two-Step Cluster Analysis

1.   INTRODUCTION

Innovative initiatives in rural areas do not arise in isolation (Esparcia, 2014), they are part of a wider process of economic and social development (Ward & Brown, 2009) and emerge from a variety of factors: the building of effective social networks and sources of information, "enlightenment" deriving from small-group interactions, and the construction of trust relations, self-help and cooperation (Ye *et al.*, 2009). Information flow in a network, depends on social embeddedness (Fritsch & Kauffeld-Monz, 2010) or social connections among members (Sorenson *et al.*, 2006), which provide opportunities for individuals to earn social benefits from the network (Thuo *et al.*, 2013). The network concept utilised widely in socioeconomic studies. Despite being a multifarious field, the key feature of network theory is its focus on relations (Marquardt *et al.*, 2012). In the context of rural change, there has been an interest in network theories for improving understanding of the complex nature of rural development (Oreszczyn *et al.*,

2010). So far, network studies have been extensively used to explain the transfer and the adoption of a new technology by farmers as a function of the position a farmer has within the network (Hermans *et al.*, 2013; Carruthers & Vanclay, 2012; Isaac *et al.*, 2007; Conley & Udry, 2001). Furthermore, a number of researchers (for example, Matuschke, 2008; Rogers, 2003) have demonstrated that the spread of new technologies within and across farming communities is related to the structure of their networks.

Many researches agree that social contacts, social interaction and interpersonal communication are important factors in the diffusion of information and knowledge, as well as in adopting new attitudes (Nair *et al.*, 2010; Goldsmith & Desborde, 1991). In fact, people before making any decision, often attempt to fortify their choice through "assenting acceptance" by some specific persons that have important influence on them and on the other members of the community in which they live in (Hazeldine & Miles, 2010). Among these particular individuals there are some that have a greater influence on the decisions of the rest and they are called "leaders of (public) opinion" or "opinion leaders" (Rogers, 1995). Network studies, identify opinion leaders based on their central position in networks defined by who turns to whom for information or advice (Iyengar *et al.*, 2011). Opinion leaders have been described as representative word-of-mouth influencers, and their influence is known to have a great impact on the decision-making process of other people.

The term was initially introduced by Lazarsfield (1944), during the presidential election of 1940 in the United States of America, when he realized that relatives, friends and colleagues exercise major influence in the choice of voting. According the "two stages flow" theory (Lazarsfeld & Katz, 1955), the people of a community are much more influenced by their interaction with other individuals than they are by the mass media, as the "opinion leader" functions as an intermediate link between the mass media and the rest of the community. In general, opinion leaders are defined as the people who have the greatest influence on their acknowledgment or adoption by other people. Having a central, well-connected position allows them to reach and influence more people. Valente & Pumpuang (2007), extend the definition of opinion leaders to their influence on the opinions, attitudes, beliefs, motivations, and behaviors of others. Whereas Rogers (2003), states that opinion leadership is *"the degree to which an individual is able to influence other individuals' attitudes or overt behavior informally in a desired way with relative frequency."* Over the last years, there has been a significant increase in the study of networks (Kilduff & Tsai, 2006; Sparrowe *et al.*, 2001), particularly with regard to their implications for leadership processes such as informal leadership (Balkundi & Harrison, 2006; Mehra *et al.*, 2006; Carroll & Teo, 1996). It is worth noting at this point that "opinion leaders" are not "leaders" in the full meaning of the term, as the leadership that they show is usually informal, they are not necessarily in charge of social organizations and they do not occupy institutional positions in the local society (Watts & Dodds, 2007).

The influence of opinion leaders has been examined in several disciplines including psychology, business and community development and has resulted in a rich literature revealing the various styles of successful leadership. However, there is a research gap in regards to the rural and agricultural context (McGehee *et al.*, 2015). When examining the general subject of agricultural extension, farmers identified as opinion leaders are an extremely valuable tool, because when detected and properly used they can render the offered programs widely accepted, thus contributing in the successful conclusion of such efforts (Siardos, 1997a). In addition, the existence of a distinguishable group of farmers-leaders, who will take actions so as to be regarded by the rest as credible and as able to give advice, is of greater importance than the application of programs of financial support towards the overall development of rural areas (Chamala & Hossain, 1996). In that way, networking has a particular utility in the construction of rural development strategies provides also, a theoretical explanation and empirical test of leadership.

This paper stems from the aforementioned discourse and tries to answer a critical question; whether people labeled (by others) as opinion leaders in a rural area evaluate themselves as such. In other words, how do we portray an opinion leader in agriculture. This study is one of the very few in the literature to categorize farmers, specifically in a cooperative, according to their "self-evaluating leadership" and this is the main contribution of the paper providing also a theoretical and methodological platform for further research.

2.   METHODOLOGICAL FRAMEWORK

A field -case study- research was carried out in a typical Greek agricultural cooperative, located in the Region of Central Macedonia (northern parts of Greece). The region comprises of seven separate Prefectures and is a typical rural area with great agricultural activity. The specific cooperative was selected as having a specific feature˙ almost all the farmers of the local community are members of the cooperative. The research started in January 2015 with a preliminary focus group with twenty farmers, divided into two separate groups. They were set up randomly without any intentional effort of affecting the "differentiality" during the selection of the members of each group. The purpose of the focus group discussion was to establish (also with the outcome of the literature review) the questionnaire for the quantitative research that would follow from April to May 2015. The latter took place in two stages.

During the first stage, farmers/members of the cooperative were involved in a sample survey in order to determine the degree of their «leadership» (self-evaluated opinion leadership techniques). Necessary adjustments were made in order to adapt the questionnaire to the particular goals of the research (Oppenheim, 1992; Siardos, 1997b). Our sampling framework was the list kept by the administrative office of the local agricultural cooperative and simple random sampling was applied onwards. For the needs of this specific research, the minimum necessary sample was set to 152 farmers/members and was selected in random until the completion of the required number, in order to have a span of trust of 95% and mean acceptable error of +/-5%. Afterwards, in order to obtain information on individual-specific networks, we asked each farmer/member to name persons to whom he or she talks most frequently when it comes to agricultural decisions. This approach is defined as the sociometric method to measure network links (Rogers, 2003). The advantage of restricting a farmer to name persons is that he or she will probably name the strongest network members, which ensures that the researcher gets a close picture of the individual network (Matuschke & Qaim, 2009) and can also visualize it (Thuo *et al.*, 2013).

In the second stage, in-depth semi –participant observation was used to disclose the local leadership network and map the central positions within this network (recommended opinion leadership). Actually, qualitative research has gained momentum as a mode of inquiry. It could be said that qualitative research generally, and into leadership in particular, is a large and rapidly expanding corpus of research. Conger (1998), argued that quantitative research alone cannot produce a good understanding of leadership, given *"the extreme and enduring complexity of the leadership phenomenon itself"* (Parry *et al.*, 2014). The qualitative research took place during August 2015, with the method of in-depth interviews and the help of an interview guide, which was based on the relevant literature and consist the driver during the interviews.

Primary data of both the quantitative and in-depth field researches have been codified and analyzed using the Statistical Package for Social Sciences (SPSS, v.22 for Windows). Initially, using a Two-Step Cluster Analysis (TSCA), the sample was stratified in some discrete clusters depending on the degree of «self-evaluated leadership» of each farmer and according to the generalizations of the related theories and based on 18 items derived from the literature and according to our aims. TSCA is a statistical analysis tool that aims to identify clusters of similar observations from a large number of ones on the basis of group categorical and/or continuous variables (attributes), by conducting statistical tests of independence of variables and tests the regularity of distribution of continuous variables and multinomial distribution of categorical ones (reference). Having accepted the consistency of the eighteen items, the average levels of agreement for each respondent for the several variables of leadership degree were used as the numerical values of the dependent variable "self-evaluated leadership". More specifically, the dependent variable "leadership degree" is a quantified multi-thematic variable (continuous) comprised of the mean values of each one of the eighteen parameters. According to the Likert 5-scale (5=strongly agree, 4=agree, 3=neither agree nor disagree, 2=disagree and 1=strongly disagree) there are five levels of agreement for each one of the leadership degree. Thus, a high value of the dependent variable expresses a positive and strong leadership loading.

Furthermore, a Categorical Regression (CatReg) model was employed, to the results of TSCA, in order to investigate in depth the possible relations among the variables of the study and to explain the clustering results. CatReg is also known as regression with optimal scaling (Meulman *et al.*, 2001; Siardos, 2005), which is an extension of classical statistical linear regression analysis technique used when some of the variables are not numeric or suspected that the relationship between variables is not linear (Siardos, 2005). CatReg quantifies data of categorical variables by assigning numerical values in categories, with a view to optimum linear regression of transformed variables (Kooij & Meulman, 1997). The next stage of the multivariable statistical analysis is about the inquiry of possible relations between the demographic and other characteristics of the farmers and their degree of "self-evaluated leadership". This is achieved by using Categorical Regression Modeling via SPSS v.22 for Windows (Michailidis *et al.*, 2010; Michailidis *et al.*, 2011; Charatsari *et al.*, 2012; Loizou *et al.*, 2013). The independent variables are presented in detail below (Table 1).

Table 1. Selected independent variables

Independent variables	Type
1. Age	Nominal
2. Marital status	Nominal
3. Annual family income	Ordinal
4. Succession of profession	Binary
5. Direction of production	Nominal
6. Number of cultivated hectares	Numeric
7. Number of own cultivated hectares	Numeric
8. Disposal of participation in an agricultural education program	Ordinal
9. DSLuse	Ordinal
10. Internet use for information on agriculture issues	Ordinal
11. e-mail use	Ordinal
12. Years of cooperative action	Numeric
13. Candidacy for Local or Municipal Council of area (present/past)	Binary
14. Member of the Cultural Association of the area (present/past)	Binary
15. Member of the Association of Parents and Guardians (present / past)	Binary
16. Taking risk for application of innovative agricultural practices	Ordinal

3. DATA ANALYSIS AND RESULTS

According to the sample summary statistics **(Table 2)** the typical farmer/member (mean participant) of the case study is male, 36-55 years of age, married with 2 children, with a low education (less than 6 years). His main employment is that of a full-time farmer and he is occupied solely with vegetative production cultivating an agricultural land of 4 ha, half of which is rented. He has been a member of the cooperative the past 16 years and the average family income is between 5,000€-15,000€, the great part of which is originating from the farm sector.

Table 2. Description of the sample (mean farmer)

Variables		Number of farmers/members	Percentage
Gender	Male	137	90,1%
Age	36-55 years	99	65,1%
Marital status	Married	123	80,9%
Number of household members	4	Mean value: 2,13 children	
Educational level	Low education	82	53,9%
Main profession	Full time farmer	141	92,8%
Succession of profession		143	94,1%
Farms	Vegetative production	132	86,8%
Annual family income	5,000€-15,000€	105	69,1%
Percentage of farming income	100%	122	80,3%
Years of occupation as a farmer		Mean value: 20 years	
Cooperative action		Mean value: 16 years	
Size of agricultural land		Mean value: 4 ha/2 ha	

The results of Two Step Cluster Analysis for the classification of farmers according to their degree of "self-evaluated leadership", led to five clusters with different farmers' profiles **(Fig. 1)**. Therefore, the cluster which showed the largest value in the distribution can be labelled as "opinion leader" (4th cluster). The next value in the distribution can be labelled as "potential opinion leader" (5th cluster), the "early majority" is the 3rd cluster of the distribution, the 1st cluster relate the "late majority" and the farmers of the 2nd cluster, can be described as "opinion laggards" or "followers" (Rogers, 2003).

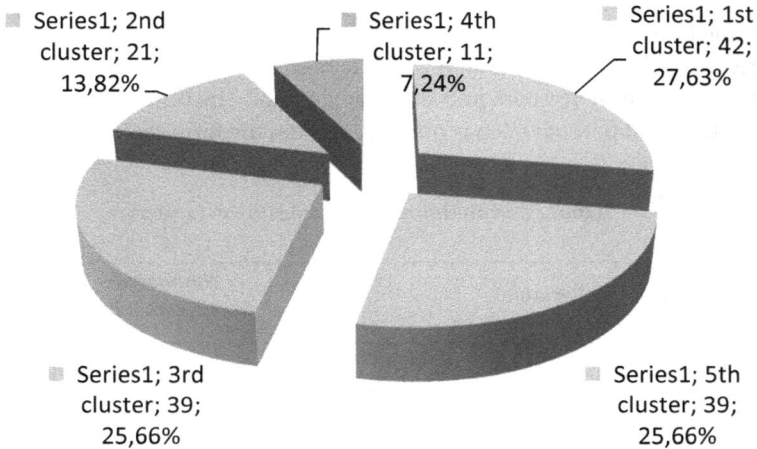

Figure 1. Segmentation of farmers according to the degree of "self-evaluated leadership"

Investigating further the degree of "self-evaluated leadership", in order to find out how it is influenced by personal characteristics, categorical regression model was employed. The CatReg model yielded a value of coefficient of multiple determination $R^2=0.952$, which indicates that 95.2% of the variance of the transformed values of the dependent variable explained by the transformed values of the independent variables of the regression equation. While examining the relative importance measures of the independent variables (Pratt, 1987) that refer to the degree of "self-evaluated leadership" **(Table 3)**, the relative importance of independent variables show that the most influential factors predicting "self-evaluated leadership", correspond to "number of own cultivated hectares" (accounting for 22%), followed by "number of cultivated hectares" (17.6%), "years of cooperative action" (13.9%) and "candidacy for Local or Municipal Council of area (present/past)" (10.6%). The presentation of the results is narrowed only of the relative importance measures, while the dependant variable cumulatively explained by the above independent variables by 64.1%.

Table 3. Relative importance measures (Correlations and Tolerance)

Independent variables	Type
1. Age	Nominal
2.Marital status	Nominal
3.Annual family income	Ordinal
4.Succession of profession	Binary
5.Direction of production	Nominal
6.Number of cultivated hectares	Numeric
7.Number of own cultivated hectares	Numeric
8.Disposal of participation in an agricultural education program	Ordinal
9.DSLuse	Ordinal
10.Internet use for information on agriculture issues	Ordinal
11.e-mail use	Ordinal
12.Years of cooperative action	Numeric
13.Candidacy for Local or Municipal Council of area (present/past)	Binary
14.Member of the Cultural Association of the area (present/past)	Binary
15.Member of the Association of Parents and Guardians (present / past)	Binary
16.Taking risk for application of innovative agricultural practices	Ordinal

Dependent variable: Degree of self-evaluated leadership

Afterwards, in-depth field research was used to disclose the local leadership network and in order to find out who holds the central positions within that network ("recommended opinion leaders"). So, all the farmers/members were asked about the person or persons who they address to for an agricultural issue they don't know and want information about it. In this way, the dominant leadership forms of the cooperative arose. In particular, farmers/members indicated the agriculturist of the cooperative as a person with a central position in the leadership network. **Table 4** presents in detail the central positions of this leadership network, as well as, the frequencies of them. It is worth noting that, "agriculturists outside of the cooperative" and "agriculturists of General for Rural Economy & Veterinary of Region" were not joined in the field research because the sample did not name them and maybe referred to more than one person. We also observe that, the leadership network of the cooperative is not confined within the formal framework (administrative & working). This finding is of high importance, as it is not about official leadership, as well as, two farmers/members of cooperative were not shown in the network due to their institutional role in cooperative, such as previous cases but it is about informal leadership.

Table 4. Leadership network

Dominant leadership forms	*Frequency*
1. Agriculturist of cooperative	107
2. Agriculturists outside of the cooperative	44
3. President of Administrative Council of cooperative	38
4. Secretary employee of cooperative	24
5. Agriculturists of General for Rural Economy & Veterinary of Region	5
6. Treasurer of Administrative Council of cooperative	2
7. Secretary of Administrative Council of cooperative	2
8. Farmer/member of cooperative (1)	2
9. Farmer/member of cooperative (2)	2

From an agricultural extension's point of view, the profile of the "recommended opinion leaders" in comparison with the profile of "mean farmer" is of great importance. Similarities were found on individual and economic characteristics and differences on professional and educational characteristics. One of the main research objectives was to rank and value several characteristics of leadership in a scale of twenty-four levels where 1=first choice and 24=last choice. In particular, "recommended opinion leaders" have been asked to rank these characteristics in the scale of **Fig. 2** and then a mean rank score extracted for each characteristic using simple frequencies and means. According to the following Figure, "Sincerity" is the most important characteristic of leadership with 4.7 mean rank score. What follows is "Integrity" (5.4), "Strong will" (6), "Humility" (6), "Authenticity" (7.14), "Ability to achieve objectives" (7.4), "Honesty" (7.71), "Vision" (8.29) and the rest are less important characteristics for the "recommended opinion leaders". These scores are very important for the quantitative modelling of the leadership. Using these scores, we can correct the general value of leadership taking into account the differences in the importance (weights) of each characteristic.

More important
1. Sincerity (4.7)
2. Integrity (5.4)
3. Strong will (6)
4. Humility (6)
5. Authenticity (7.14)
6. Ability to achieve objectives (7.4)
7. Honesty (7.71)
8. Vision (8.29)
9. Confidence (9.6)
10. Ambition (9.71)
11. Decision making ability (11.6)
12. Communication skills (12)
13. Sensitivity foe fellowman (12.3)
14. Convince (14)
15. Reputation (14.4)
16. Guts (15.1)
17. Active (15.3)
18. Emotional intelligence (17.3)
19. Tactician (17.9)
20. Discipline (18)
21. Centralization (18)
22. Efficacy (18)
23. Enforcement (20)
Less important
24. Loneliness-Need for isolation (23.6)

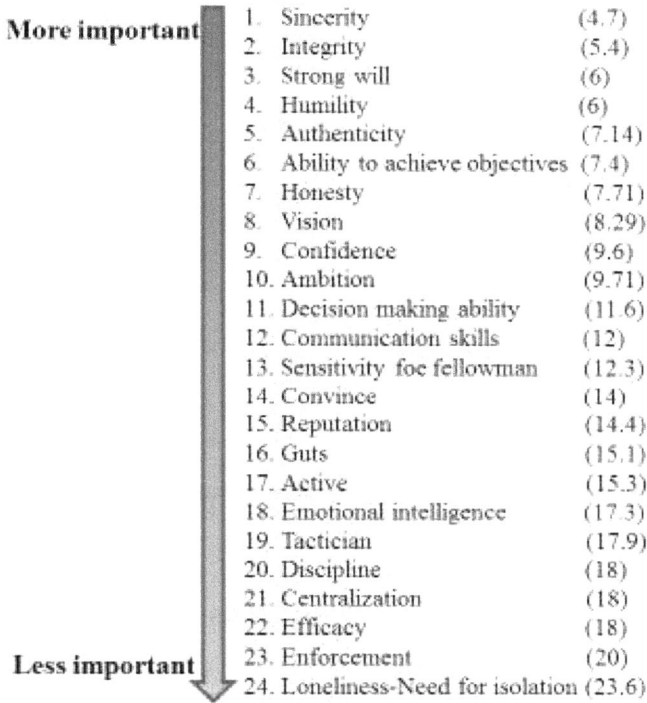

Figure 2. Leadership characteristics (ranking)

Finally, in order to address the critical question of this paper; whether people labeled (by others) as opinion leaders in a rural area evaluate themselves as such, descriptive statistics was used into the cluster of "self-evaluated opinion leaders" (4th cluster) and were compared with the "recommended opinion leaders" which arises from the leadership network of the agricultural cooperative. This description/methodology has helped us to find out the common ground between "self-evaluation" and "by recommendation" leadership and in fact to approach the "real" leader-farmer. According to the following Figure 3, among the seven "recommended opinion leaders" who participated in the second round of personal interviews, only one appears in both categories of leadership and this person is the president of the agricultural cooperative who actually is the "real" leader influencing other farmers/members of the cooperative. Thus, there is no significant relationship between "self-evaluation" and "by recommendation" leadership.

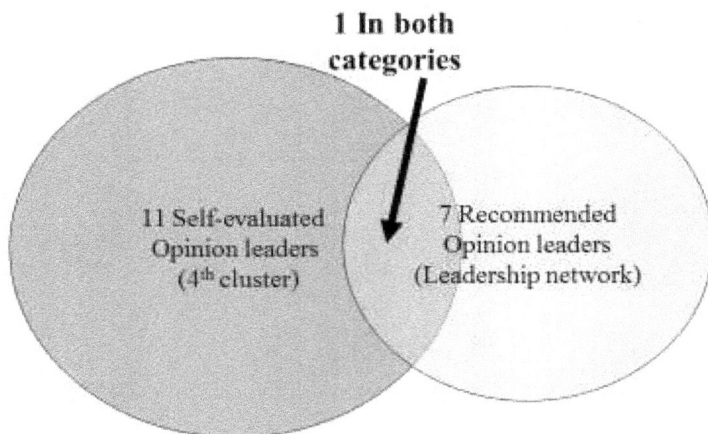

1 In both categories

11 Self-evaluated
Opinion leaders
(4th cluster)

7 Recommended
Opinion leaders
(Leadership network)

**Figure 3. Relation between "self-evaluation" and "by
recommendation" leadership**

4.   CONCLUSIONS

This paper sheds light to a difficult topic that is the identification of the opinion leader portrait in agriculture (specifically within members of a cooperative). The first part of this research led to the investigation networking of farmers/members, providing a guide of identification of the "opinion leaders" ("by recommendation"), so that they can be potentially used as "intermediates" of agricultural politics and as "tools" of influence over the rest of the farmers and mainly over the "opinion laggards". Let us not forget that these farmers, when discovered and efficiently used, offer the ability of wide acceptance of offered programs and thus contribute to the successful end of such efforts. In addition, it is noted the usefulness of network analysis to understanding the mode of operation (interaction of farmers) of an agricultural cooperative. The knowledge resulting from this analysis, can be used for the adoption/diffusion of an innovation through the central position ("recommended opinion leaders") as suggested by the leadership network. Moreover, the existence of a distinctive group of leading farmers that are acting in such a manner that the rest of them will regard them as credible and as worthy of taking counsel from, is of greater importance for the evolution of rural areas than the application of a program of financial support.

The next goal of this research was the determination of the "leadership degree" of the sample. The Two-Step Cluster Analysis, led to the segmentation of farmers based on the dependent variable "degree of self-evaluated leadership" in five discrete clusters according to the generalizations of the related theories. Exploring the critical question of this paper, we concluded that the approach was used is an indication that those who consider themselves as "opinion leader" does not necessarily mean that it is.

Methodologically, the combination of qualitative and quantitative research allows the estimation of "leadership" of farmers, offering a security control of surveying the process of evaluating. In the same time, the combined application of the Two-Step Cluster Analysis and of the Categorical Regression allows for the segmentation of farmers, as well as, the discovery of the factors that shape the forenamed segmentation.

However, when examining the situation having in mind the agricultural applications, one can make certain that there is need for further exploration of farmers' "leadership degree", as it is shown by the results of this research. A further quantitative and qualitative research in a number of agricultural cooperatives and with the use of larger focus groups could contribute towards this goal. Also, visualizing farmers' networks illuminates some of the supports and constraints that directly impact investments in agriculture. Among the main drawbacks of the research are the following: (a) lies mainly in the subjectivity of the evaluation process that concerns the appraisal of the "leadership degree" amongst the sample of farmers/members, (b) within the limitations one must take into consideration the research to a single cooperative and the small sample and (c) the absence of women from the sample. Women farmers were excluded from positions within the agricultural cooperative-the gender stereotype conflicts with the leadership stereotypes. Hence results must be evaluated within the aforementioned limitations. More empirical studies, especially in rural areas, which analyzing networks in detail can improve the understanding of social learning in adoption decisions and can help policy makers to develop more targeted strategies to promote agricultural innovations and rural growth. Still the dominant place of the president of the agricultural cooperative in Greece exerts his role as being "the one", the one who will influence people, the one to whom farmers are turning to in order to get advice. It seems that he is the one, but will he be also the one to drive them to innovation amidst such an inconsistent environment?

REFERENCES

Balkundi, P. & Harrison, D. (2006). Ties, Leaders, and Time in Teams: Strong Inference about Network Structure's Effects on Team Viability and Performance. Academy of Management Journal, 49, pp. 49–68.

Carroll, G.R. & Teo, A. C. (1996). On Social Networks of Managers. Academy of Management Journal, 39, pp.   421–440.

Carruthers, G. & Vanclay, F. (2012). The Intrinsic Features of Environmental Management Systems that Facilitate Adoption and Encourage Innovation in Primary Industries. J. Environ. Manage. 110, pp. 125–134.

Chamala, S. & Hossain, S.M.A. (1996) Adoption of formal agricultural credit by opinion leaders and other farmers in differentially developed villages of Bangladesh, Savings and Development, 20(4): 431-445.

Charatsari, C., Papadaki-Klavdianou, A. and Michailidis, A. (2012). Farmers as consumers of agricultural education services: Willingness to pay and spend time. Journal of Agricultural Education and Extension, 17(3), 253-266.

Conley, T. & Udry, C. (2001). Social Learning through Networks: the Adoption of New Agricultural Technologies in Ghana. Am. Agric. Econom. Assoc. 83 (3), pp. 668–673.

Esparcia, J. (2014). Innovation and Networks in Rural Areas. An Analysis from European Innovative Projects. Journal of Rural Studies, 34, pp. 1-14. European Innovative Projects. Journal of Rural Studies, 34, pp. 1-14.

Fritsch, M. & Kauffeld-Monz M. (2010). The Impact of Network Structure on Knowledge Transfer: An Application of Social Network Analysis in the Context of Regional Innovation Networks. The Annals of Regional Science, 44 (1), pp. 21-38.

Goldsmith, R.E. & Desborde R. (1991). A Validity Study of a Measure of Opinion Leadership. Journal of Business Research, Vol. 22, pp. 11-19.

Hazeldine, M.F. & Miles, M.P. (2010). An Exploratory Role Analysis of Opinion Leaders, Adopters, and Communicative Adopters with a Dynamically Continuous Innovation. Journal of Applied Business Research,   26(4), pp. 117 130.

Hermans, F., Stuiver, M., Beers, P.J. & Kok, K. (2013). The Distribution of Roles and Functions for Upscaling and Outscaling Innovations in Agricultural Innovation Systems. Agricultural Systems, vol. 115, pp. 117-128.

Isaac, M.E., Erickson, B.H., Quashie-Sam, S.J. & Timmer, V.R. (2007). Transfer of Knowledge on Agroforestry Management Practices: The Structure of Farmer Advice Networks. Ecol. Soc. 12 (2).

Iyengar, R., C. Van den Bulte, J. Eichert, B. West, & T.W. Valente (2011). How Social Networks and Opinion   Leaders Affect the Adoption of New Products. New Theories, Vol. 3.

Kilduff, M. & Tsai, W. (2006). Social Networks and Organizations. London, England: Sage Publications.

Kooij, A.J. van der & Meulman, J.J. (1997). MURALS: Multiple Regression and Optimal Scaling using Alternating Least Squares in Bandilla W. and Faulbaum E. (eds), Softstat '97.

Lazarsfeld, P. & Katz, E. (1955). Personal Influence. Cambridge, MA: Harvard University Press.

Lazarsfeld, P. (1944). Radio and the Printed Page: An Introduction to the Study of Radio and Its Role in the Communication of Ideas. New York: Duell, Sloan, and Pearce.

Loizou, E., Michailidis, A. and Chatzitheodoridis, F. (2013). Investigating the drivers that influence the adoption of differentiated food products: The case of a Greek urban area. British Food Journal, 115(7), 917-935.

Marquardt, D., Möllers, J. & Buchenrieder, G. (2012). Social Networks and Rural Development: LEADER in Romania. Sociologia Ruralis, vol. 52, no. 4, pp. 398 431.

Matuschke, I. & Qaim, M. (2009). The impact of social networks on hybrid seed adoption in India. Agricultural Economics (40) pp. 493-505.

Matuschke, I. (2008). Evaluating the Impact of Social Networks in Rural Development Systems: An Overview. Washington D.C.: International Food Policy Research Institute.

McGehee, N.G., Knollenberg, W. & Komorowski, A. (2015). The Central Role of Leadership in Rural Tourism Development: A Theoretical Framework and Case Studies. Journal of Sustainable Tourism.

Mehra, A., Dixon, A.L., Brass, D.J. & Robertson, B. (2006). The Social Network Ties of Group Leaders: Implications for Group Performance and Leader Reputation. Organization Science, 17, pp. 64–79.

Meulman, J. J., Heiser, W. J. and SPSS (2001). SPSS Categories 11.0, Chicago: SPSS Inc.

Michailidis, A., Koutsouris, A. and Mattas, K. (2010). Information and communication technologies as agricultural extension Tools: A survey among farmers in West Macedonia, Greece. Journal of Agricultural Education and Extension, 16(3), 249-263.

Michailidis, A., Partalidou, M., Nastis, S.A., Papadaki-Klavdianou, A. and Charatsari, C. 2011. Who goes online?   Evidence of internet use patterns from rural Greece. Telecommunications Policy, 35(4), 333-343.

Nair, H.S., Manchanda, P. & Bhatia, T. (2010). Asymmetric Social Interactions in Physician Prescription Behavior: The Role of Opinion Leaders. Journal of Marketing Research, 47(5), pp. 883-895.

Oppenheim, A. (1992) «Questionnaire Design, Interviewing and Attitude Measurement». Printer, London and Washington.

Oreszczyn, S., Lane, A. & Carr, S. (2010). The Role of Networks of Practice and Webs of Influencers on Farmers' Engagement with and Learning about Agricultural Innovations. Journal of Rural Studies, vol. 26, no. 4, pp. 404 417.

Parry, K., Mumford, M.D., Bower, I. & Watts, L.L. (2014). Qualitative and Historiometric Methods in Leadership Research: A Review of the First 25years of the Leadership Quarterly. Leadership Quarterly, vol. 25, no. 1, pp. 132-151.

Pratt, J.W. (1987). Dividing the indivisible: using simple symmetry to partition variance explained. In Proceedings of the second International Conference in Statistics, ed. T. Pukkika and S. Puntanen, 245-260. Tampere.

Rogers, E. (1995). Diffusion of Innovations. (4th ed.), New York, NY: The Free Press.

Rogers, E.M. (2003). Diffusion of Innovations. 5th Ed. New York: Simon & Schuster.

Siardos, G. (2005) «Multivariate statistical analysis». Vol. 2: third edition, Athens: Stamoulis

Siardos, G. (1997a) «Agricultural Extension». Thessaloniki: Ziti

Siardos, G. (1997b) «Methodology of social research». Thessaloniki: Ziti

Sorenson, O., J. Rivkin, & L. Fleming. (2006). Complexity, Networks and Knowledge Flow. Research Policy 35, pp. 994-1017.

Sparrowe, R., Liden, R., Wayne, S. & Kraimer, M. (2001). Social Networks and the Performance of Individuals and Groups. Academy of Management Journal, 44, pp. 316–325.

SPSS (2015). SPSS Categories 22.0 and User Manual. Chicago: SPSS Inc.

Thuo, M., Bell, A.A., Bravo-Ureta, B.E., Okello, D.K., Okoko, E.N., Kidula, N.L., Deom, C.M. & Puppala, N. (2013). Social Network Structures among Groundnut Farmers. Journal of Agricultural Education and Extension, vol. 19,   no. 4, pp. 339-359.

Valente, T.W. & Pumpuang P. (2007). Identifying Opinion Leaders to Promote Behavior Change, Health Educ. Behav. 34 (6) pp. 881–896.

Ward, N. & Brown, D.L. (2009). Placing the Rural in Regional Development. Reg. Stud. 43 (10), pp. 1237-1244.

Watts, D.J. & Dodds, P.S. (2007). Influentials, Networks and Public Opinion Formation. Journal of Consumer Research, Vol. 34, pp. 27-36.

Ye, J., Wang, Y. & Long, N. (2009). Farmer Initiatives and Livelihood Diversification: From the Collective to a Market Economy in Rural China. Journal of Agrarian Change, vol. 9, no. 2, pp. 175-203.

Chapter 3

STUDYING THE ICT MANAGEMENT OF AGRI-FOOD SECTOR ON SUPPLY CHAIN LEVEL – THE FIRST STAGE: ANALYSIS OF AGRICULTURAL ICT USAGE

János Felföldi[1], Szilvia Botos[2], Ádám Péntek[3], Róbert Szilágyi[4] and László Várallyai[5]

[1]*University of Debrecen, Faculty of Economics and Business, Institute of Applied Informatics and Logistics*
H-4032 Debrecen, Böszörményi út 138,
felfoldi.janos@econ.unideb.hu

[2]*University of Debrecen, Faculty of Economics and Business, Institute of Applied Informatics and Logistics*
H-4032 Debrecen, Böszörményi út 138,
botos.szilvia@econ.unideb.hu

[3]*University of Debrecen, Faculty of Economics and Business, Institute of Applied Informatics and Logistics*
H-4032 Debrecen, Böszörményi út 138,
pentek.adam@econ.unideb.hu

[4]*University of Debrecen, Faculty of Economics and Business, Institute of Applied Informatics and Logistics*
H-4032 Debrecen, Böszörményi út 138,
szilagyi.robert@econ.unideb.hu

[5]*University of Debrecen, Faculty of Economics and Business, Institute of Applied Informatics and Logistics*
H-4032 Debrecen, Böszörményi út 138,
varallyai.laszlo@econ.unideb.hu

ABSTRACT

The agriculture and the processing of agricultural products have an important role in the Hungarian economy. The SME sector is especially important to the overall Hungarian economy and there is also a key role of SMEs in the Hungarian agro-food sector. Our research concept is originally based on the assumption that there is a substantial gap in usage of ICT tools in business relations of actors in the agribusiness chain. Agricultural enterprises, both holdings and small farms are vital part of the chain, but in the case of ICT usage, small and medium-sized agricultural enterprises might be key players in information gap. In the case of agro-food SMEs, those ICT tools which used for tracing the products – and which must be used in many cases in accordance with food safety legislations – not only provide information for food safety but for management and this information could be vital for smooth the material flows and for maintain continuity of information flows which could increase the efficiency and reduce costs. The overall objective of our research is to explore the characteristics of using ICT tools in the partnerships and internal processes of enterprises throughout the whole agro-food supply chain. In order to achieve this objective, the first step of our research to find out these features of agricultural enterprises by analyzing their situation among other SMEs. In our recent article, we show the role of food industry in the Hungarian economy and the result of our questionnaire regarding to the usage of ICT of SMEs, highlighting the situation of agricultural enterprises, their gaps and potential in the agribusiness chain. The competitiveness of the SME sector in Hungary is on the wane both within the EU and internationally. Comparing to EU-28 average, the performance of Hungarian SME sector has gradually worsened between 2008 and 2015. Regarding the ICT usage, the situation of the overall SME sector in the Northern Great Plain is at a low level, but at least agro-enterprises is not lagging behind the enterprises of other sectors in terms of the level of usage the modern internet-based services. Regarding the possible explanatory variables, results demonstrated that there is no substantial difference among the enterprises by activity but the size class of the enterprises has influence, the higher the size of the enterprise, the higher the probability of use these services. It is worth preparing the agro-enterprises to use the new and in many cases free ICT services for their activity as according to the technology acceptance model they are generally lagging behind.

KEYWORDS

Agriculture, SME, ICT, agro-food, supply chain.

JEL CLASSIFICATION CODES

L86, M15, Q13

1. INTRODUCTION

The agro-food supply chains are highly complex system involving multiple actors in both horizontal and vertical dimension, they are built on many partnerships and cooperation forms and consists of heterogeneous processes and systems (Wolfert et al., 2010b; Kaloxylos et al., 2013). Based on literature search there is direct and demonstrable link between performance indicators which generate profit (e.g. customer and supplier satisfaction or the costs of storage and transport) and ICT usage. High level of information management is also crucial in the agro-food supply chains because these solutions can help the actors to operate more efficiently by transparent and continuous flow of information. Agro-food businesses in the chain from production to processing must therefore use ICT because an informational gap could put all the stakeholders in the chain at a competitive disadvantage. But the level of usage is also important, because between actors (raw material suppliers, raw material producers, processors, distributors, retailers and consumers) it could be so different which impede the effective operation and development of businesses.

Our research covers the ICT usage of all stakeholders in the chain, taking into account that all actors have two sides within the chain, the supply and demand side and they use differently ICT tools with them. Our concept is originally based on the assumption that there is a substantial gap in usage of ICT tools in business relations of actors in the agribusiness chain so we focus on the usage of ICT in different flows among the actors of the agro-food chain (material, information, money) and in their relationships but drink sector is excluded. The first stage to reach our aim is analyzing the main features of ICT use in agricultural enterprises by analyzing their situation among other SMEs[7].

Agricultural enterprises, both holdings and small farms are vital part of the chain, but in the case of ICT usage, small and medium-sized agricultural enterprises might be key players in information gap. Therefore, their usage characteristics of different ICT tools and mainly the safe and fast, Internet-based cloud services should be unfolded to show them how they could use ICTs and make information an instrument which increasing efficiency in their supplier and customer relations.

We deal with the agricultural sector in this paper so we will present the importance of food supply chain industry in general, highlighting in particular the role of agriculture in the chain and the situation of SME and agricultural sector in the Hungarian economy, their gaps and potential in the agribusiness chain. Our results represent the usage trend of modern ICT tools in the Hungarian SMEs on

---

[7] SMEs: in the article the term SMEs (Small and Medium Sized enterprises) also includes micro enterprises

regional level (Northern Great Plain) and the position of agricultural enterprises among them.

2. LITERATURE REVIEW

There are several aspects to analyze the food supply chain depending on which part of the chain is studied. There are three main actors in the chain: the agriculture, the processing sector of food and drink and the distribution and retail sector. On Figure 1 the parts and actors of food supply chain can be seen with the major flows among the actors.

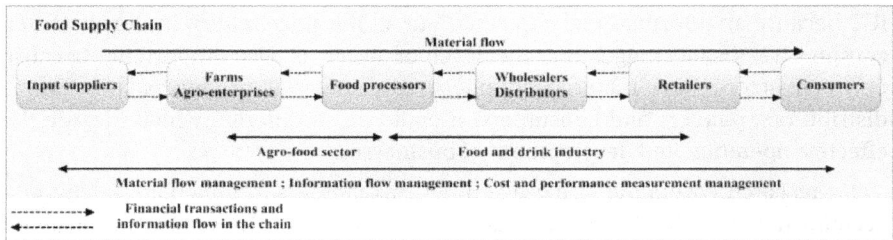

Figure 1. The general linear structure and parts of Food Supply Chain
Source: Own editing on Pullman & Wu, 2012; Berti & Mulligan, 2015

Together, the agricultural sector, the food and drink industry (processing and manufacturing) and the distribution sector (wholesale and retail) are the driving forces of the food supply chain. There is no single, homogeneous, and common food supply chain at European level. The length and the degree of complexity of food supply chains depend on the product and market characteristics (European Commission, 2015a).

As regards the different parts of food supply chain we can talk about two major types of industries: the food and drink industry and the agro-food industry. The food and drink industry includes all the processed products values and the retail sector. The agro-food industry is centered on making, processing, preparing and packaging food products for human consumption. Its raw materials come from the primary sector, specifically from agriculture (Barcelona Treball, 2013). In the case when a research focuses on the business relationships within the agro-food chain (including just agriculture and food and drink processing sector), agro-food business chain could also be used as define the mainstream of a study.

Agro-food enterprises operate in a complex and dynamic environment and to meet increasing demands of consumers, government and business partners, enterprises continuously have to work on innovations of products, processes and ways of cooperation in agro-food supply chain networks (Wolfert et al., 2010a). Innovations in different processes can make products more suitable for global distribution, and innovations in management and ICT allows supply chains to become more responsive to the increasingly sophisticated food demands of consumers (Dani, 2015). But one of the principal weaknesses of the Hungarian SMEs is low innovation ability (including ICT usage) and performance (Szira, 2014). The potential contribution of ICT to develop the competitiveness of SMEs has proved by many empirical studies. Bayo-Moriones & Lera-López (2007) have proved the positive impact of ICT for general business indicators like productivity, profitability, market value and market share by analyzing indirect indicators such as process efficiency, quality of service, cost savings, flexibility of organization and production and customer satisfaction. ICT help enterprises to seek business in other countries and to harmonize easier their activities with partners by using information systems even they are geographically remote from each other (Fathian et al., 2008). According to Guo & Jin (2009) the usage of ICT and e-commerce just helps survival, it does not mean economic advantage for the enterprises in a market where there is high degree of competition. If rural SMEs want to be competitive now, they need to extra services which increase the satisfaction of partners and customers and the safety of business transactions. Ericsson (2015) presented the role of ICT in transitioning to sustainable food systems and summarizes that digital technologies might be applied in all processes of the chain.

A survey of Dutch arable agro-food supply chain network was conducted by Wolfert et al. (2010a) and they concluded that developments should follow a service-oriented architecture (SOA) approach, and should support companies to focus on their business processes. Kaloxylos et al. (2013) deal with the influence of different Internet-based services in their article and they have presented the SmartAgrifood architecture that aims at building an integrated food chain that will allow data to be transferred bi-directionally in an automatic and simple way. It is important, because as Poppe et al. (2013) explain, by improving the interoperability of data which are being generated in agriculture and the rest of the food chain, the processes can be optimized and data-intensive food chains have the potential to alleviate many of the current sustainability and food safety issues. To create business process management systems using mobile or cloud technologies could allow supply chains and the stakeholders to break through in today's industry because of their significantly lower entry cost (Ericsson, 2015), but SME sector means a bottleneck in use of ICT tools for decades besides the households, mainly in rural regions (Pierson, 2005; Struzak, 2010; OECD, 2015). The uptake of ICT solutions has been slow for a number of reasons and a key challenge for ICT in the agriculture sector is information management, both within specific domains and across the whole supply chain from farm to fork (Brewster et al., 2012).

Agriculture is an important sector in the agro-food chain, so farmers are also key players in it and in the information flows. Hence, there is a need for a better assessment of the impacts of using value-added agricultural ICT services on smallholder farmers besides other actors in the food system value chain (Steinfield & Wyche, 2013). Several studies have been made on factors which has impact for ICT use of the agricultural actors. Steinfield & Wyche (2013) have analyzed the role of different socio-economic factors in the use of ICT in agriculture. They found there is relation between ICT adoption, use, and impact by age, gender, and income, among other factors. Earlier, Ali and Kumar (2011) made a study about how socio-demographic factors such as education, social category, income and landholding size are important that affect the usage of information technology in decision-making. However, in the farm sector the use of ICT technology has increased strongly over the last decade and for example the use of precision agriculture techniques has been introduced successfully in a number of European regions, especially in arable farming (Poppe et al., 2013), but regarding the advanced ICT such as Cloud services, the European enterprises have still a distrust of them which means barrier in usage (Sasvári, 2016). This fact is justified by a survey of Brewster et al. (2012) on usage of advanced internet technologies and only a few respondents used really those that are already available today, while the majority of the respondents use basic and simple systems and applications. On the other hand, recent surveys also found that agro-food SMEs are getting interested in practical, close to market applications and they started to recognize the advantages of using the Cloud. Sasvári (2016) made a comparison on Cloud Computing usage between Austrian and Hungarian enterprises and the results suggest that SMEs consider the high-level mobility and remote access to information systems while large enterprises the faster information flows as advantages.

The SME sector has obviously an essential role in the Hungarian economy, as in the agro-food sector, but its competitiveness is on the wane both within the EU and internationally (Szira, 2014). In the case of agro-food SMEs, those ICT tools which used for tracing the products – and which must be used in many cases in accordance with food safety legislations – not only provide information for food safety but for management and this information could be vital for smooth the material flows and for maintain continuity of information flows which could increase the efficiency and reduce costs. Steinfield & Wyche (2013) highlighted that it must identify both barriers and facilitators to adoption of ICT-based value-added agricultural service. Encouraging higher uptake of ICT is essential for the SME sector and policy makers have a crucial role to remove those barriers which SMEs currently face with regard to adoption of ICT (OECD, 2015). In this way the analyses of SMEs which operate in the different parts of the agro-food chain are important to determine those factors which mean obstacle for them in the exploitation of potential of ICT.

3. METHODOLOGY

In accordance with our aim by secondary data analysis we present the Hungarian agro-food industry and SME sector based on data of Eurostat, Central Hungarian Statistical Office and the FoodDrinkEurope by descriptive statistics. A survey was also performed for the assessment of ICT preparedness and usage characteristics of the micro-, small- and medium-sized enterprises.

The data for the study has been collected from 294 enterprises belonging to the Northern Great Plain region (NUTS2) of Hungary. The survey was conducted in the second half of 2015 and using structured questionnaire and responses and recorded by personally contacting the leaders or a management member of the enterprises. 4 surveys have excluded because of missing data. The enterprises have been selected by stratified sampling based on statistics of the Hungarian Central Statistical Office. The basis of sampling was the distribution of staff employed and business activity of the enterprises. Our sample well represents the distribution of Hungarian SMEs. The number of sample enterprises by economic characteristics is shown on Table 1.

Activity	Users	Non-users	Annual turnover (Ft)	Users	Non-users
Agriculture	26	20	< 50 million	64	71
Service	52	40	50-100 million	36	33
Commerce	33	46	100-500 million	18	23
Building industry	19	15	500 million - 1 billion	8	5
Other industry	20	19	> 1 billion	24	8

Staff category	Users	Non-users	Age of the leader	Users	Non-users
1-10 persons	58	71	25-35 years	23	25
11-49 persons	51	45	36-50 years	80	70
50-249 persons	41	24	> 50 years	44	48

Table 1. The economic profile of the surveyed enterprises
Source: own survey

The current investigation examined to what extent the basic features of enterprises (number of employees; annual turnover; business activity) explain an enterprise use modern ICT technology for safety communication and data storage and binary logistic regression have been used to determine it as our dependent variables are dichotomous and the independent variables are categorical and each have more than two categories. We used for the analysis the recommendations of Tranmer & Elliot (2008), King (2008) and Harrell (2015). A binary logistic regression predicts the probability that an observation falls into one of two categories of a dependent variable based on one or more independent categorical variables.

The general formula for our calculation is the following: We have 3 binary response variables (y). y_1 is the usage of free cloud service over internet, y_2 is the usage of data backup system over internet and y_3 is the usage of Virtual Private Network (VPN) service. In these series $y_i = 1$ if the answer is yes in observation$_i$ and $y_i = 0$ if the answer is no in observation$_i$. We have 4 explanatory variables (x). x_1 is the age of respondent, x_2 is the activity of branch of the enterprise, x_3 is the size of the enterprise by staff categories and x_4 is the annual average revenue. x_1 is ratio scale variable. x_2, x_3 and x_4 are nominal categorical variables. After we validated the data series for the analysis, the calculation is done for a random sample of 203 items which was 70% of the total number of sample (290 items) and for validating the result obtained for the previous sample we used the remained 30% of the sample with 87 items as Holdout subsample.

4.   RESULTS

4.1 OVERVIEW OF AGRO-FOOD AND SME SECTOR IN THE EU AND IN HUNGARY

Food production and consumption is central to any society, and has economic, social and, in many cases, environmental consequences (European Commission, 2013). In 2012 more than 24 million people were employed in the food supply chain, representing about 11% of total employed population of EU. The total turnover of the food supply chain surpassed €3,800 billion in 2012 and generated a value added of almost €680 billion (about 6% of the EU gross value added). Food spending represents about 15% of the average EU household budget (European Commission, 2015a). The detailed key data on the food supply chain in the European Union are shown in Figure 2.

Turnover		Value added	
409 € billion 11%		208 € billion 31%	
1062 € billion 28%		206 € billion 30%	
1255 € billion 33%		104 € billion 15%	
1132 € billion 29%		160 € billion 24%	
Number of employees		**Number of companies**	
11.6 million 48%		12 248 thsd 89%	
4.3 million 18%		2% 289 thsd	
2 million 8%		2% 338 thsd	
6.2 million 26%		6% 822 thsd	

○ Agriculture   ◉ Food and drink industry
◉ Wholesale of agricultural and food products   ● Food and drink retail

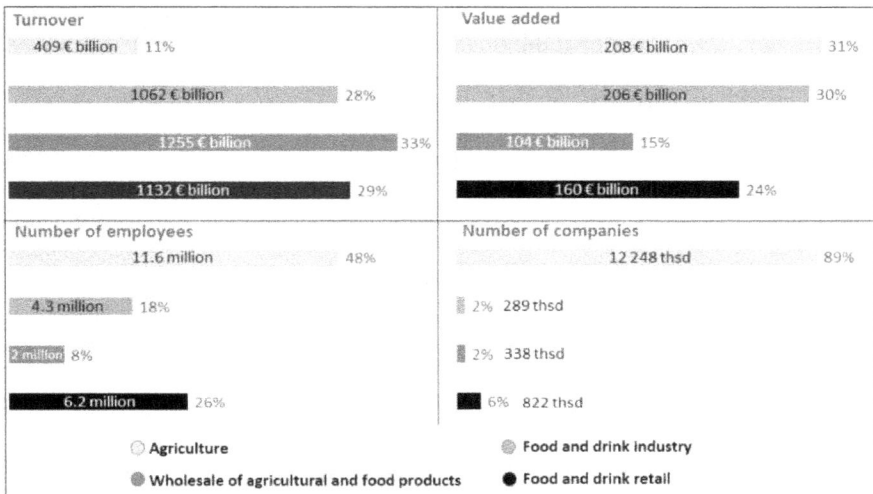

Figure 2. Distribution of key indicators in the food supply chain by actors in 2012
Data source: www.fooddrinkeurope.eu

The agro-food industry – the first part of the chain – is the second largest segment of EU: more than 12 million farms produce agricultural products for processing by about 290,000 enterprises in the food and drink industry (European Commission, 2015b).

Agro-food industry has a major importance in the Hungarian economy as well. In Hungary, 62.9% of the overall territory (9.3 million hectares) are utilized for agricultural activities. Eighty percent of the total territory of Hungary is agricultural production area. More than half (59%) of this area is arable land and around a quarter (26%) is forest. Almost 1 million farmers work in this sector and there are over 5,000 registered food businesses in the country. On recent statistics 7-8% of the population works full time in agriculture and for another 4% it means supplementary income. Hungarian agriculture produces 3.4% of GDP and contributed 49% to the national economy's trade surplus in 2014. Agricultural products were responsible for 9.2% of exports within the national economy, and 6% of imports. The expenditure for food and non-alcoholic beverages from the total annual living expenditure (per capita) is 23.1% in Hungary (HCSO, 2014; Flanders, 2015).

SME sector is also especially important to the overall Hungarian economy as they mean 99.9% from the total operating enterprises, it provides jobs for 73.8% of the employees in business sector and they produce about 50% of the Gross Value Added (HCSO, 2015). In the Hungarian agro-food sector SMEs also have a key role. 98% of the agricultural holdings are SMEs however they use just 36% of the agricultural land. They represent almost the half of the total amount of agricultural standard output and 84% of agricultural employees are directly employed by small and medium-sized holdings. The contribution of different sizes of holdings to the Hungarian agriculture sector is shown on Figure 3. Unlike the standard SME classification due to the different economical features of holdings, the categories have been determined by agricultural size of the farms in respect of the Hungarian conditions. In this way, we classified farms having less than 10 hectares as micro holdings, farms having 10-50 hectares of agricultural area as small sized holdings; farms with 50-100 hectares as medium sized holdings and farms having more than 100 hectares as large holdings.

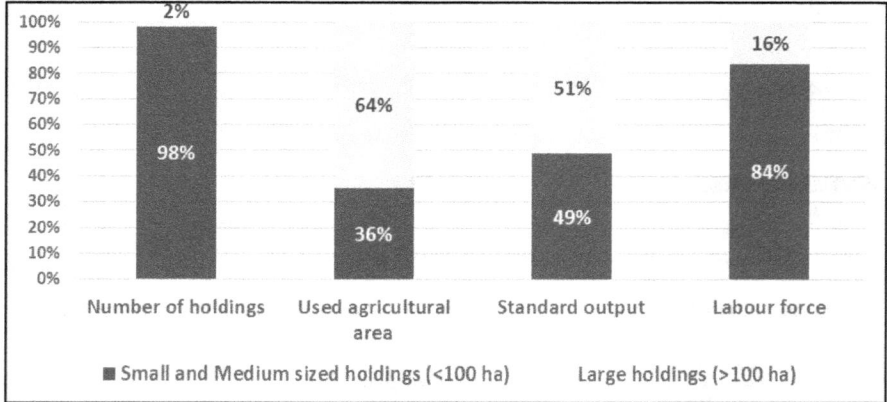

Figure 3. Contribution of holdings to agriculture by size in Hungary, 2013
Data source: Eurostat, 2014

The features of SMEs operating in food and drink industry is similar to the agricultural contribution structure. According to Hungarian Statistical Agency, in 2013 the number of agro-food enterprises was almost 5% of the total number of enterprises operating in the Hungarian economy (HCSO, 2013). The characteristics of SMEs in the Hungarian food and drink industry is shown on Figure 4.

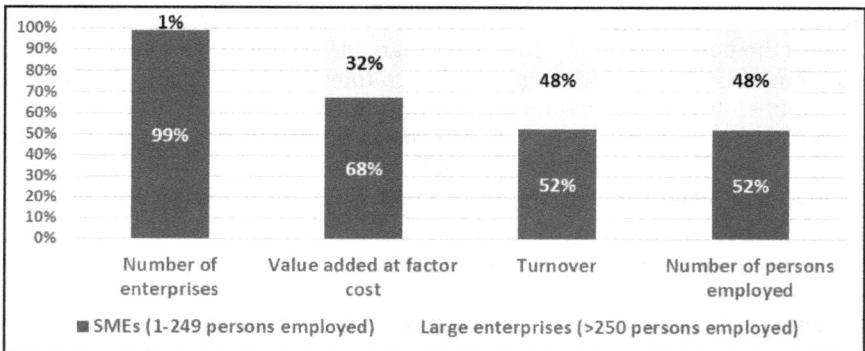

Figure 4. Contribution of enterprises to the food and beverages industry by size in
Hungary, 2013
Data source: Eurostat 2014

Regarding the tendency of performance of the SME sector, comparing to EU-28 average, the performance of Hungarian SME sector has gradually worsened between 2008 and 2015 as shown in Figure 5.

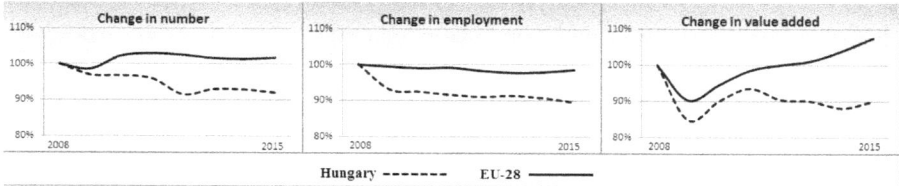

Figure 5. The change of the performance of Hungarian SMEs compared to EU-28 between 2008 and 2015
Source: HCSO, 2016

According to Eurostat (2014) the situation of Hungarian SMEs (10-249 persons employed) regarding to use of Cloud services is under the average of EU-28. Our position is very poor even the average usage ratio is low in other Member States as well. 18% of SMEs buy cloud computing services over the internet in EU-28 while in the case of Hungarian SMEs this ratio is just 8%. The tendency is similar in other indicators like usage of Customer Relationship software or usage of cloud service for safety data storage or communication.

In summary, the agro-food processing industry means higher added value and thus it contributes to the GDP in higher proportion than the simple production of primer agricultural products. The sector has a key importance even in compared to the other EU-members' food industry, so keeping and developing the competitive advantage is crucial.

4.2 USE OF ADVANCED ICT IN THE SME SECTOR – A REGIONAL CASE STUDY

A survey was performed for the assessment of ICT preparedness and usage characteristics of SMEs, highlighting the situation of agricultural enterprises. The sample origins from 290 enterprises belonging to the Northern Great Plain region of Hungary. The survey contained questions about how the enterprises use ICT for their activities mainly for their general administration procedures and internal and external communication. We analyzed to what extent the basic features of enterprises (number of employees; annual turnover; business activity) explain an enterprise use modern ICT technology for safety communication and data storage. The result of the calculation can be seen in Table 2.

Variables (x)	B	S.E.	Wald	Sig.	Exp(B)	95% C.I for EXP(B) Lower	Upper
Usage of Cloud services							
Number of employees	0,397	0,248	2,569	0,109	1,487	0,915	2,416
Branch of activity	0,002	0,112	0,000	0,985	1,002	0,805	1,248
Age of the leader	-0,010	0,016	0,366	0,545	0,991	0,960	1,022
Annual revenue	-0,057	0,125	0,212	0,645	0,944	0,740	1,206
Constant	-0,593	0,785	0,570	0,450	0,553		
Usage of data back-up systems							
Number of employees	0,872	0,290	9,064	0,003	2,391	1,356	4,218
Branch of activity	-0,067	0,135	0,246	0,620	0,935	0,718	1,218
Age of the leader	0,000	0,019	0,000	0,995	1,000	0,963	1,038
Annual revenue	0,032	0,140	0,051	0,810	1,032	0,785	1,358
Constant	-2,737	0,999	7,508	0,006	0,065		
Usage of VPN							
Number of employees	0,142	0,417	0,116	0,734	1,153	0,509	2,610
Branch of activity	0,099	0,172	0,335	0,563	1,105	0,789	1,547
Age of the leader	0,006	0,026	0,059	0,809	1,006	0,957	1,058
Annual revenue	0,606	0,168	12,963	0,000	1,833	1,318	2,549
Constant	-4,430	1,420	9,728	0,002	0,012		

Table 2. Result of Binary Logistic Regression – Variables in the Equation

The values in column "B" tell information about the relationship between the independent and dependent variables which could be positive or negative, so they sign the amount of increase or decrease in the case of a 1 unit changing. For the independent variables where coefficients are about 0 are not significant. Column of "S.E." means the standard errors associated with the coefficients and it is used for testing whether the parameter is significantly different from 0. Columns labelled "Wald" and "Sig." tell whether the coefficients are statistically significant. The column "Exp(B)" contains the odds ratios for the predictors. They are the exponentiation of the coefficients. The Sig. column contains the 2-tailed p-value for each independent variable and on the basis of the value and preselected Alpha-value (0,05 in our calculation) can be decided if the null hypothesis can reject or not. Those coefficients are statistically significant which have a p-value of 0.05 or less.

On the basis of p-value the Number of employees is a significant factor (Sig=0,003) in the case of Usage of data back-up systems (y_2) and Annual revenue is a significant factor (Sig=0,000) in the case of Usage of VPN (y_3). There is a slight effect (Sig=0,109) of Number of employees for Usage of Cloud services (y_1).

The Branch of activity and the Age of the leader were not included to the explanatory variables. It means that agro-enterprises is not lagging behind enterprises with activities in terms of the level of use modern internet-based services. In the case of y1 and y2 we analyzed also the differences between categories and the results demonstrated the influence of the size class of the enterprises: the higher the size of the enterprise, the higher the probability of use these services.

5. CONCLUSION

Agro-food industry has a major importance in the Hungarian economy and the sector has a key importance even in compared to the other EU-members' food industry, so keeping and developing the competitive advantage is crucial. Regarding to use Cloud services, our position is very poor even the average usage ratio is low in other Member States as well and the tendency is similar in other indicators like usage of Customer Relationship software or usage of cloud service for safety data storage or communication.

Regarding the usage of different internet-based ICT tools, there is no substantial difference among the enterprises by activity. In general terms, the intensity of ICT usage is unfortunately low in the overall SME sector in the Northern Great Plain, but at least agro-enterprises is not lagging behind the enterprises of other sectors in terms of the level of use these services. It is worth preparing the agro-enterprises to use the new and in many cases free ICT services for their activity as according to the technology acceptance model they are generally lagging behind.

In our future research, we will conduct survey in agro-enterprises with size of small and medium (10-249 persons employed) as the size of the enterprises is in correlation with usage of ICT. Considering their number, they can be the greater part of suppliers of food processors and in this way, we can determine a business model as a best practice for agricultural enterprises in their relation with food processors. As applications which popular in private sector are not in more common usage in the SME sector yet, it is important to analyze in detail the ICT usage characteristics of agro SMEs in the food supply chain because these ICT devices, tools and services are crucial to smooth the information flow within the chain. The further step in our research to find out why they do not use internet services and what they use instead of them for their daily administration, communication and performance measurement.

REFERENCES

Ali, J. and Kumar, S. 2011. Information and communication technologies (ICTs) and farmers' decision-making across the agricultural supply chain. *International Journal of Information Management*. Volume 31. pp. 149-159.

Barcelona Treball, 2013. Agro-Food Industry – Sector Report 2013. Available at: http://w27.bcn.cat/porta22/images/en/Barcelona_treball_Informe_sectorial_A gro_food_industry_gen2013_en_tcm43-4016.pdf

Bayo-Moriones, A. and Lera-López, F., 2007. A firm-level analysis of determinants of ICT adoption in Spain. *Technovation*. Volume 27. Issue 6-7. June-July 2007. pp. 352-366.

Brewster, C. et al., 2012. Identifying the ICT challenges of the Agri-Food sector to define the Architectural Requirements for a Future Internet Core Platform. *Proceedings eChallenges e-2012*, Lisbon, Portugal. pp. 1-8.

Dani, S., 2015. *Food Supply Chain Management and Logistics – From Farm to Fork*. Kogan Page, London, Philadelphia, New Delhi.

Ericsson, 2015. *ICT & the Future of Food and Agriculture. Industry Transformation – Horizon Scan: ICT & the Future of Food*. Telefonaktiebolaget LM Ericsson, Stockholm, Sweden.

European Commission, 2013. Healthier Animals and Plants and a Safer Agri-Food Chain A modernised legal framework for a more competitive EU. Available at: http://eur-lex.europa.eu/legal-content/EN/TXT/?uri=CELEX%3A52013DC0264

European Commission, 2015a. Background on the EU food supply chain: an important economic sector. Available at: http://ec.europa.eu/competition/sectors/agriculture/overview_en.html

European Commission, 2015b. You are part of the food chain – Key facts and figures on the food supply chain in the European Union. EU Agricultural Market Briefs. No. 4. Available at: http://ec.europa.eu/agriculture/markets-and-prices/market-briefs/pdf/04_en.pdf

Eurostat databases

Fathian, M. et al., 2008. E-readiness assessment of non-profit ICT SMEs in a developing country: The case of Iran. *Technovation*. Volume 28. Issue 9. September 2008. pp. 578-590.

Flanders Investment & Trade, 2015. *Agro & Food Sector in Hungary*. Flanders Investment & Trade, Budapest, Hungary.

FoodDrinkEurope, 2015. Data & Trends. *European Food and Drink Industry 2014-2015*. FoodDrinkEurope, Brussels, Belgium

Guo, Q. and Jin, B., 2009. Development of E-business and Networking in Rural Small and Medium-sized Enterprises. *Information Science and Engineering (ICISE)*. Nanjing, China, pp. 2912-2915.

Harrell, F. E. Jr., 2015. Regression Modeling Strategies, Chapter 10 – Binary Logistic Regression. Springer International Publishing, Switzerland.

Hungarian Central Statistical Office (HCSO) databases

Kaloxylos, A. et al., 2013. The Use of Future Internet Technologies in the Agriculture and Food Sectors: Integrating the Supply Chain. *Procedia Technology*. Volume 8. pp. 51-60.

King, J. E., 2008. Binary Logistic Regression. In: Best Practices in Quantitative Methods. Edited by Jason Osborne. SAGE Publications, Los Angeles, USA

OECD, 2015. *OECD Digital Economy Outlook 2015*. OECD Publishing, Paris, France.

Pierson, J. 2005. The take-up of ICT by micro-enterprises: An assessment of the bottlenecks and of European initiatives. *Communication & Strategies*, No. 57. 1st quarter. p.25.

Poppe et al., 2013. Information and Communication Technology as a Driver for Change in Agri-food Chains. *EuroChoices* Volume 12. Issue 1. pp. 60- 65.

Pullman, M. and Wu, Z., 2012. *Food Supply Chain Management – Economic, Social and Environmental Perspectives*. Routledge, New York, USA.

Sasvári, P., 2016. The analysis of the knowledge and use of Cloud Computing among enterprises in Austria and Hungary. *Gradius* Volume 3 Issue 1 pp. 478-484.

Steinfield, C. and Wyche, S., 2013. *Assessing the Role of Information and Communication Technologies to Enhance Food Systems in Developing Countries*. Global Center for Food Systems Innovation ICT4D White Paper, Michigan State University, East Lansing USA.

Struzak, R., 2010. Broadband Internet in EU Countries: Limits to Growth. *IEEE Communication Magazine*. Volume 48. Issue 4. April 2010. pp. 52-57.

Szira, Z., 2014. *The situaton of the SME sector in Hungary*. In: Management, Enterprise and Benchmarking – In the 21st Century. Econpapers, Budapest, Hungary. pp. 107-118.

Tranmer, M. and Elliot, M., 2008. Binary Logistic Regression. Cathie Marsh for Census and Survey Research, Manchester, United Kingdom.

Wolfert, S. et al., 2010a. Organizing information integration in agri-food – A method based on a service-oriented architecture and living lab approach. *Computers and Electronics in Agriculture*. Volume 70. pp. 389-405.

Wolfert, S. et al., 2010b. Information Sharing & ICT in Agri-Food Supply Chain Networks – a view from different perspectives. *ICT-ENSURE*, Paris, France.

IDENTIFYING MARKET STRATEGIES FOR GREEK SPECIALTY PRODUCTS IN THE UNITED STATES

Liliana Almonte[1], Tyler Leighton[1], Sarah Rogers[1], Pabitra Saikee[1], Nicola Bulled[1] and Robert Hersh[1]

[1]*Worcester Polytechnic Institute, Interdisciplinary and Global Studies Division, 100 Institute Road, Worcester, MA USA, nbulled@wpi.edu*

ABSTRACT

Purpose – Stagnant sales of specialty food items within the domestic market in Greece have increased the need for small-scale artisanal food businesses to seek new markets abroad. 'Marianna's Vineleaves,' a small, family-owned enterprise in Thessaloniki, Greece, is one such business looking to expand its international exports of viticulture products, such as stuffed vine leaves – ntolmadakia.

Design/methodology/approach – Using a mix method approach, we assessed United States consumer preferences towards Greek specialty food products and examined existing promotional strategies. We hypothesize that food related lifestyle clusters, socioeconomic and demographic characteristics, or a combination, influences product purchasing preferences.

Findings – Employing multiple and varied strategies to assess consumer preferences results in a nuanced approach to marketing artisanal food products in a new market. Results from taste tests, focus group discussions, pile sort exercises, and a survey revealed that using words such as 'healthy' and 'Mediterranean' motivates U.S. consumers to purchase artisanal foods at higher prices. Packaging aesthetics, such as clear labels, easy to read fonts, limited colors, tags and twine convey high-end, quality, and authenticity. Finally, providing information shifts attitudes towards novel products, such as Marianna's Vineleaves ntolmadakia, which can motivate consumption.

Research limitations/implications – The small and geographically limited sample used in this study limits the generalizability of findings. The same research methodology could be applied to a larger and more diverse sample to assess not only a single product's packaging, but overall perceptions of Greek artisanal food products.

Originality/value – The study used a unique combination of research methods to identify key marketing strategies to direct the actions taken by Greek specialty food producers interested in entering the United States market.

KEYWORDS

Alphabet theory; artisanal products; consumers; food-related lifestyle clusters; Greek specialty foods; market behavior

JEL CLASSIFICATION CODES

D4, L660

1. INTRODUCTION

Assessing consumers' food choices is challenging given the large number of factors that affect purchasing decisions (Lappalainen, Kearney, & Gibney, 1998). Food consumers can be segmented according to lifestyle, a mixture of habits, conventional ways of doing things, and reasoned behavior (Nie & Zepeda, 2011). Consumer behavior is also driven by socioeconomic factors and demographics. By understanding food buying motivations, specialty food producers can classify and segment market clusters and develop appropriate marketing strategies for a competitive advantage (Rong-Da Liang & Lim, 2011).

'Marianna's Vineleaves,' a small, family-owned enterprise in Thessaloniki, Greece, seeks to expand its specialty food exports, specifically *ntolmadakia* (stuffed vine leaves) to the United States market. Once a backyard business, Marianna's Vineleaves has developed a reputation for its quality artisanal food products throughout Thessaloniki and the northern Greece region. This family business now aspires to enter a larger market, joining the "new, rising trend" of Mediterranean cuisine, which has consistently outperformed categories such as 'ethnic food' as a growing sector of interest in the U.S. (Organization for Economic Co-operation and Development, 2014). However, adequate market intelligence concerning consumer preferences and the marketing strategies successfully employed by competing producers is needed.

We assess consumer motivations for Greek specialty food products and currently employed promotional elements in order to guide marketing strategies of small family owned business enterprises like Marianna's Vineleaves. The following questions guide the study:

1. What motivates consumers to purchase and consume Greek specialty food products?

2. How can product packaging direct specialty foods buying practices?

2. RESEARCH

2.1. WHAT MOTIVATES CONSUMERS TO BUY SPECIALTY FOODS?

Consumers are driven by numerous and varied factors when purchasing and consuming food products. Extensive research in the area of food market segmentation indicates that attitudinally based variables such as perceptions around the product quality, the producer, the freshness of the ingredients, have far greater influence on food selection habits than socioeconomic factors, knowledge, or context (Cranfield, Henson, & Blandon, 2012). Cranfield, Henson and Blandon (2012) note that "attitudes rather than socioeconomic factors … make it difficult to distinguish easily consumers; [as such], we have to delve into the broader attitudes of consumers to begin to understand the appeal … and how these attitudes must be changed if the consumption of such products is to be promoted." Attitude variables are identified as related to lifestyle, reflecting general and observable values and characteristics of consumers (Demby, 1974; Wells, 1975). Segmenting the food market by lifestyle is often combined with a clustering approach to identify consumers as whole persons rather than isolated fragments (Plummer, 1974). Research has identified five food-related lifestyle (FRL) clusters: adventurous, rational, careless, conservative, and uninvolved food consumers (Nie & Zepeda, 2011).

According to the FRL approach, for each of these lifestyle clusters, five components explain food-purchasing habits: ways of shopping, quality aspects, cooking methods, consumption situations, and purchasing motives (O'Sullivan, Scholderer, & Cowan, 2005; Scholderer, Brunsø, Bredahl, & Grunert, 2004). Consumer lifestyle clusters vary in their preferences with regards to these indicated components; see Table 1. For example, the adventurous consumer values the social aspects of food, including cooking and eating with friends or family. Convenience is of little importance, while value for money, health, taste, freshness, and organically produced foods are more important, as compared to other consumer segments. One could hypothesize that these consumers are more likely to purchase specialty food products. Conservative consumers, on the other hand, are resistant to trying anything new; this is likely to include specialty food products (Lone & Bech, 2001). Conceptualizing the specialty food market in this manner, as lifestyle clusters, provides one approach to understanding the attitudes and motivations of consumers (Nie & Zepeda, 2011).

Table 1. Five food-related lifestyle (FRL) consumer groups and their traits (Lone & Bech, 2001; Wycherley, McCarthy, & Cowan, 2008)

Type of Consumer	Traits
The Adventurous Food Consumer	• Greatest interest in food, including specialty foods. • Enjoys eating out and with friends. • Not interested in convenience. • Interested in cooking, looks for new ways to cook and involve the whole family in the cooking process. • Regards health, quality, taste, freshness and value for money to be important.
The Rational Food Consumer	• Has planned meals and shopping. • Regards product information to be important. • Enjoys shopping and uses a shopping list. • Enjoys meal preparation more than other segments. • Not convenience oriented. • Regards health, quality, taste, freshness and value for money to be important.
The Careless Food Consumer	• Least interested in shopping. • Little or no interest in cooking. Most emphasis on quick and easy cooking. • Least likely of all segments to plan their meals and shopping in advance. • Least interested in basically all food quality aspects.
The Conservative Food Consumer	• Traditional in their attitudes towards cooking and shopping. • Least interested in organic foods or anything new, such as specialty food. • Most price conscious. Value for money is important. • Carefully plans meals and shopping.
The Uninvolved Food Consumer	• Uninterested in food and anything food related such as shopping, eating specialty food etc. • Attach little importance to quality, taste, price and freshness when purchasing food. • Least interested in cooking. Emphasize on quick and easy cooking. • Don't plan their meals.

Although "ambiguous" (Cranfield et al., 2012) in their role in influencing food choices, socioeconomic and demographic factors such as age, gender, income, and regional background should still be considered. A survey study of 137 males in the United States National Guard conducted by Tepper and colleagues (1997), examined the effect of socioeconomic or demographic variables on selected food choice, as well as restrained eating, nutrition knowledge, and beliefs about selected foods. The findings indicated a negative correlation between age and soda consumption (r=-0.07, p<0.05), and a positive correlation between income and meat consumption (r=0.112, p<0.05). Additional studies indicate that place of residence influences consumptions of 'healthy' foods. Participants living in a rural area were less likely to consume healthy foods as compared to those in a suburban area (Tepper, Choi, & Nayga, 1997). In a study conducted among 358 adults in the U.S. by Steptoe and colleagues (1995), a difference in how consumers rate food on a 'health scale' by gender was assessed using a Food Choice Questionnaire. Women appeared to pay more attention to how healthy a food product is as compared to men. As these studies indicate, while food market segmentation by lifestyle clusters offers a holistic perspective of consumers, the influence of socioeconomics on food preferences should not be dismissed.

Finally, the consumer markets for specialty foods are likely to present unique characteristics as compared to general food market segments. The desire to try new things is a significant motivation to experiment with unusual and costly foods (Purcell, 2015). In addition, specialty foods are seen as higher quality and healthier than other standard food items (Purcell, 2015). Consequently, some consumers perceive specialty foods as a treat, or a reward for good behavior, justifying the higher cost, but a self-indulgence to be enjoyed in small portions, in moderation, or only on occasion (Wycherley, McCarthy, & Cowan, 2008). Research also suggests that consumers desire new experiences in eating; a craving satisfied through the consumption of specialty foods from new and different food cultures (DataMonitor, 2005; Vignali-Ryding, Sanchez, & Vignali, 2003). Collectively, this evidence suggests that intentions to purchase specialty food products depend, to some degree, on how the product meets and satisfies the needs and desires of the consumer (Lai, 1991) and is not limited to specific FRL clusters. In fact, consumers who purchase specialty foods may be overlap multiple FRL clusters or be distinct from FRL clusters.

In this light, strategies to identify, understand, predict, and motivate specialty food consumers require a more comprehensive and nuanced approach. One approach, known as the Alphabet Theory, considers consumers' attitudes, values, beliefs, and norms collectively as a way to predict food-purchasing behavior, as informed by information/knowledge about the food product, context related to where the consumer both purchases and eats the food making the food exotic or mundane, and consumer socioeconomics (including age, gender, and class), see Figure 1. As these elements have been found essential in describing food consumption, Alphabet Theory was selected as a framework for this study. It also provides an opportunity to explore interactions between different elements, namely attitudes, values, information seeking, and demographics, which might prove useful in drawing conclusions about how to market specialty food products.

Figure 1. Conceptual framework of Alphabet Theory (modified from Zepeda & Deal, 2009)

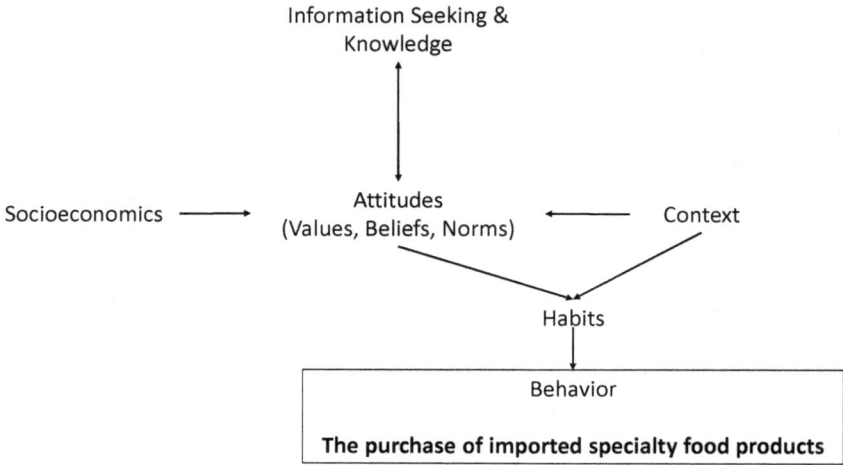

2.2. HOW CAN PRODUCT PACKAGING DIRECT SPECIALTY FOODS BUYING PRACTICES?

Understanding the elements that motivate specialty food buying behaviors allows for more targeted marketing strategies, including product packaging (Wang, 2013). Packaging can provide visual and verbal cues that attract attention, provide information, and set expectations (Silayoi & Speece, 2007), which can be directed at specific market clusters or consumer characteristics. Visual package elements are known to play a significant role in affecting consumer-buying decisions, especially in low-involvement products such as routine purchases like milk and eggs (Silayoi & Speece, 2004). Packaging shape, color, graphics, and layout have been shown to have stronger influence on purchasing decisions than either convenience or product information, collectively accounting for almost 75% of the likelihood to buy (Silayoi & Speece, 2007). For example, consumers classified as 'adventurous' are likely to be attracted to products that appear unique and unusual, that stimulate the senses, and are well made and healthy. However, given that consumers are motivated by diverse factors, the impact of such packaging characteristics is likely to vary.

Consumers can be convinced to purchase food products through the manipulation of one or more packaging variables, including packaging color, clear packs that allow viewing the food within, nomenclature, and brand name appearance (Silayoi & Speece, 2007). Certain words and phrases are often used in product labeling to psychologically influence the thoughts and behaviors of consumers during the food buying process (Northup, 2014). Recent work in cognitive and social psychology has demonstrated that some judgments, including food purchases, may be particularly sensitive to the cognitive context (Herr, 1989). In this regard, priming, or the activation of a concept using specific words to influence thoughts and behaviors (Northup, 2014), can be applied to food product packaging. For example, in a study of food products available in major supermarkets in the United Kingdom, the word 'Mediterranean,' used more frequently than country/region of origin on food product packaging, influenced consumers' subjective criteria including perceptions of authenticity (Cannon, 2005). Such research indicates that producers can tailor product packaging to persuade clusters of consumers, or consumers with certain characteristics, to purchase specialty food products.

3. METHODS

The study aimed to understand attitudes towards specialty food products in order to successfully introduce international artisanal foods, specifically Marianna Vineleaves' *ntolmadakia*, to the U.S. market. We used a mixed methods approach to: (1) identify and understand factors that influence U.S. consumer preferences for specialty imported food products; and, (2) examine marketing approaches of other Greek specialty food producers in order to identify key marketing strategies.

A series of three blind taste tests were conducted with 6 Greek consumers residing in the U.S. and 20 U.S. consumers. Participants were asked to consider and record their thoughts on the taste, look, texture, and overall impression of three different *ntolmadakia* (Marianna's, Onassis, and Aegean). Participants were also asked to consider their overall perceptions or attitudes towards Greek food, generally as a free listing exercise. Free listing is one of several structured interviewing techniques designed to elicit systematic data about a cultural domain (Gravlee, 1998). Free lists contain information about how people perceive relationships between items in a domain, as items listed first are more important to individuals, and items occurring more frequently across many lists have a shared importance for the collective (Gravlee, 1998). Free listing can help understand how a domain is perceived across a group of people by examining the average psychological salience of items (Sinha, 2013).

Taste test participants were also directed to participate in a focus group discussion as a way to verbalize impressions of the *ntolmadakia* provided and general perceptions of Greek food. Focus group discussions allow for the vetting of differences in opinions, the consideration of agreements, and the reaching of a general consensus among a group of people (Bernard, 2006). Discussions explored participants' opinions of the perceived quality of the different *ntolmadakia*, the appearance of the packaging, expectations of price, and willingness to pay.

In order to identify successful key words and packaging aesthetics, we examined high-end specialty food products labels and descriptions currently available to the U.S. market. This process involved the collection of descriptions from online catalogues used by high-end distributors and retailers including *Formaggio's Kitchen, Yoleni's, Titan Foods, Trader Joes, Hellenic Farms, Christos Market,* and *Optima Foods.* In addition to examining product text descriptions, the aesthetics of the product labelling for various specialty food products were analyzed. Images of 37 specialty food products were identified to be included in a pile sorting exercise. Unconstrained pile sorting involves the placement of items (in this case images of specialty food products) into piles based on perceived shared characteristics (Weller & Romney, 1988), with participants offering descriptions as to why certain items were grouped together. Eighteen U.S. consumers completed the pile sorting. Cluster names were generated based upon the pile descriptions offered. The intention was to understand how U.S. consumers perceive aesthetic characteristics of specialty food products. Finally, a self-administered, electronic survey was administered to faculty and staff at a small private university in northeastern U.S. via an email listserv. The survey aimed to understand motivations behind specialty food consumption and consumer preferences towards key labeling characteristics for Marianna's Vineleaves *ntolmadakia.* The survey consisted of three sections: socioeconomics (6 questions), food-related lifestyle (69 questions), and three different Marianna Vineleaves' ntolmadakia labels (4 questions). The complete, validated, food-related lifestyle (FRL) instrument, as developed by Brunsø and Grunert (1995; 1998), was used in the survey. The instrument consists of 69 Likert-type items, measuring 23 dimensions, each belonging to one of five food-related lifestyle aspects: ways of shopping, quality aspects, consumption situation, cooking methods, and purchasing motives. Each dimension is measured by a three-item scale. Respondents were asked to rate their attitude towards the statements on a Likert scale, ranging from (1) 'strongly disagree' to (7) 'strongly agree.' Food-related lifestyle (FRL) aspects correspond with food cluster groups, but also reveal behaviors pertaining to the purchase of artisanal products such as shopping at specialty stores, purchasing novelty items, concerns over the healthiness of food, and the importance of taste. Marianna's Vineleaves graphic designer produced three unique labels modeled after the high-end and artisanal products. Label 1 aimed to represent a high-end design, with its minimal design, open space, small size, and transparent label. The second and third labels represented an artisanal design with spaced fonts, neutral colors, and descriptive text. The third label also incorporated modern graphics (swirls). All three labels contained the phrase "A step in the Mediterranean diet." We used PATH analysis to determine if behaviors such as 'shopping at specialty stores' and 'purchasing novelty items' are motivated by attitudes, information, context and/or socioeconomic factors, as suggested by the Alphabet Theory (Zepeda and Deal, 2009). Path analysis, a form of structural equation modeling allows for the assessment of relationships between multiple variables simultaneously (Kline, 2005).

3.1. DATA ANALYSIS

Text analysis was conducted on the blind taste test tasting descriptions of the ntolmadakia, resulting in the formulation of a codebook. The codebook also contained words from the free-listing exercise of general perceptions of Greek food. All text data (focus group discussions, free lists, and product descriptions) were coded using the developed codebook. Frequency and salience index scores were calculated on free lists words. Salience measures take into account the open-ended nature of free listing, and incorporate both how often and how early items occur in respondents' lists. Pile sorting data was analyzed using cluster analysis (multidimensional scaling) to assess the relative closeness of items, or likelihood of one item appearing in the same pile as another pile, across participants. The process revealed related product clusters. From these clusters, key labeling and design components were assessed to identify particular characteristics unique to each cluster's theme. Through this process, labeling elements used by various high-end brands were identified. Qualitative data (free lists and pile sorts) were analyzed using ANTHROPAC version 1. The survey was created and administered using Qualtrics Research Suite. Univariate and multivariate analyses (one-way ANOVA, Pearson's correlations and path analyses) were conducted on the 111 returned surveys (4.58% response rate), using SAS v9.2.

4. RESULTS

Taste testing revealed that 80.7 percent of the participants had eaten *ntolmadakia* before. Out of the 26 participants, 11 preferred Aegean (commonly available in local supermarkets, produced in China, 4.00USD), eight preferred Marianna's Vineleaves, and six preferred Onassis (purchased at specialty food store, produced in Greece, 5.00USD). However, preferences varied when examined by demographic cluster. Of young U.S. consumers (n=10), 90 percent preferred Aegean. Young Greeks residing in the U.S. (n=6), the most familiar with *ntolmadakia*, all preferred Onassis. An older demographic of U.S. consumers (n=10) preferred Marianna's Vineleaves (80 percent).

The free listing exercise aimed to identify concepts U.S. consumers associate most with Greek food. The terms healthy (0.519), Mediterranean (0.278), fresh (0.239), tasty (0.214), and oily (0.121) had the highest salience scores. Text analysis of product descriptions of *ntolmadakia* already available in the U.S. market revealed six commonly used descriptors: Greek, tender, soft, fresh, and specialty.

Considering the overlap of free list terms on general perceptions of Greek food and descriptors of marketed *ntolmadakia* revealed specific terms that producers, such as Marianna's Vineleaves should consider when marketing to U.S. consumers: healthy, Mediterranean, and fresh.

Focus group discussions revealed additional perceptions related to the perceived quality of *ntolmadakia* products, the packaging, and consumers' willingness to pay. Discussions related to the product container, the organic nature of the vineleaves, the product's origin, color, and taste indicated particular product characteristics that consumers valued. Marianna's Vineleaves *ntolmadakia* are sold in a glass jar, which many participants appreciated. Participants liked seeing the product through the jar, noting that, "it felt almost more personal...[to] see [the product]." Glass jars were perceived to be healthier and of "higher quality." Most *ntolmadakia* available in the U.S. are packaged in cans. Although the vine leaves used in Marianna's *ntolmadakia* are organic, this did not alter participants taste preferences or intention to purchase; however, it did alter willingness to pay. All participants agreed that they automatically perceive organic to be more expensive, with one participant stating, "I would tack on a couple more dollars for organic." Overall, participants were willing to pay between 3.00 and 8.00 USD per jar, with the older demographic willing to pay more (5.61 USD) than the younger demographic (5.25 USD). Most participants were unaware of the origin of the *ntolmadakia* included in the taste test, referencing the interchangeable use of the terms 'Greek' and 'Mediterranean.' Given that *ntolmadakia* are part of many food cultures, participants believed the products could be from Lebanon, the Middle East, or Europe.

Consumers distinguish product aesthetics based on preferences for particular marketing attributes. Using cluster analysis (multidimensional scaling) to assess the pile sorting of images of Greek products available in the U.S. market, six thematic clusters emerged: high-end, elegant, artisanal, modern, homemade, and cheap (see Figure 2). Each cluster has unique design characteristics, including distinct fonts and font sizes, size and transparency of product package, and graphics. For example, 'high-end' products have a simply shaped container and minimalist label design (often transparent), colors are neutrals and light, font is large and easily legible, graphics (if used) are abstract and modern, and containers are glass. 'Artisanal' product packaging is also simple and minimal in design, using a neutral color palette and modern abstract graphics, but with the addition of homemade touches like yarn around the lid and tags with more explanation of the product, its production, or the history of the business.

Figure 2. Multidimensional Scaling clusters of Greek specialty food product packaging

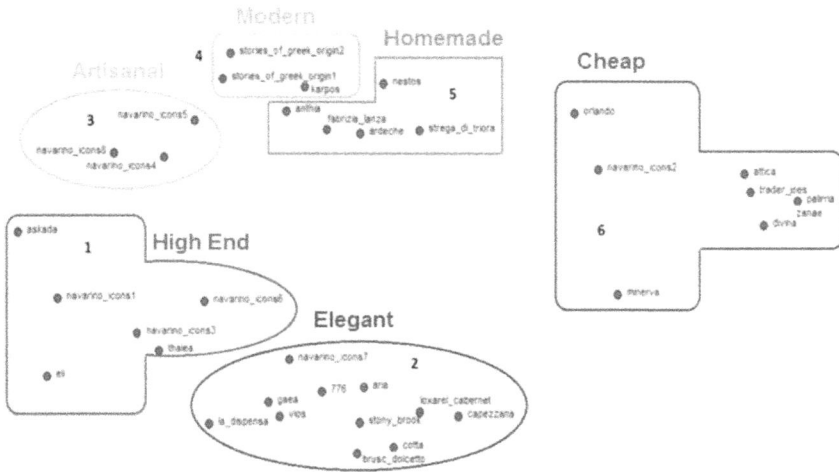

Based on the literature, we hypothesized that consumer preferences for product packaging and label design would vary. Adventurous consumers may be drawn more to a label characterizing high-end qualities, while rational and conservative consumers more drawn to a label characterizing artisanal qualities. However, other characteristics, as indicated by alphabet theory, may motivate purchasing decisions. The survey was developed as a way to assess this. Survey respondents were 61.3% female; a mean age of 35.2 years old; 38.7% reported a household size of two people; a household income of between 100,000 and 200,000 USD (39.6%); and graduate level education (64.9%), see Table 2. Characterized into their food lifestyle cluster using the FRL instrument (Cronbach's α = 0.815) 53.2% of respondents were conservative, 25.2% rational, 10.81% careless, 6.30% adventurous, and 4.50% uninvolved.

Table 2. Socioeconomics of survey respondents

Demographic	Item	Total (n=111)	Adventurous (n=7)	Rational (n=28)	Conservative (n=59)	Careless (n=12)	Uninvolved (n=5)
Gender	Male	43 (38.7%)	4 (57.1%)	8 (28.5%)	27 (45.7%)	3 (25%)	1 (20%)
	Female	68 (61.3%)	3 (42.8%)	20 (71.4%)	32 (54.2%)	9 (75%)	4 (80%)
Age	20-29	26 (23.4%)	5 (71.4%)	3 (10.7%)	16 (27.1%)	1 (8.3%)	1 (20%)
	30-39	16 (14.4%)	1 (14.2%)	4 (14.2%)	8 (13.5%)	2 (16.6%)	1(20%)
	40-49	23 (20.7%)	0	11 (42.8%)	9 (15.2%)	3 (25%)	0
	50-59	25 (22.6%)	0	7 (25%)	13 (22.0%)	4 (33.3%)	1(20%)
	60+	21 (18.9%)	1(14.2%)	3 (10.7%)	13 (22.0%)	2 (16.6%)	2 (40%)
Education	High school	7 (6.30%)	1(14.2%)	0	5 (8.4%)	1 (8.3%)	0
	Undergraduate	32 (28.8%)	2(28.5%)	7 (25%)	15 (25.4%)	5 (41.6%)	3(60%)
	Graduate	72 (64.9%)	4(57.1%)	21 (75%)	39 (66.1%)	6 (50%)	2(40%)
Household Size	1	14 (12.6%)	1(14.2%)	3 (10.7%)	9 (15.2%)	1 (8.3%)	0
	2	43 (38.7%)	3 (42.8%)	7 (25%)	27 (45.7%)	4 (33.3%)	2(40%)
	3	17 (15.5%)	1(14.2%)	5 (17.8%)	9(15.2%)	1 (8.3%)	1(20%)
	4	23 (20.7%)	1(14.2%)	10 (17.8%)	6 (10.1%)	4 (33.3%)	2(40%)
	5	10 (9.00%)	1(14.2%)	2 (7.1%)	6 (10.1%)	1 (8.3%)	0
	6	2 (1.80%)	1(14.2%)	0	1(1.6%)	0	0
	7	3 (2.70%)	0	1 (3.5%)	1(1.6%)	1 (8.3%)	0
Income	< $50,000	15 (13.5%)	2 (28.5%)	1 (3.5%)	11(18.6%)	1 (8.3%)	0
	$50,001-75,000	10 (9.1%)	1 (14.2%)	2 (7.1%)	5 (8.4%)	1 (8.3%)	1(20%)
	$75,001-100,000	20 (18.0%)	2 (28.5%)	7 (25%)	7 (11.8%)	3 (25%)	1(20%)
	$100,001-200,000	44 (39.6%)	2 (28.5%)	11(39.2%)	25 (42.3%)	5 (41.6%)	1(20%)
	$200,000+	22 (19.8%)	0	7 (25%)	11(18.6%)	2 (16.6%)	2 (40%)

One-way ANOVA analyses indicate that certain FRL dimensions related to artisanal food products such as *ntolmadakia*, including shopping at specialty stores, concerns over the healthiness of food choices, and taste are influenced by socioeconomic characteristics. Younger individuals expressed greater enjoyment of shopping (F=2.329, p=0.061). Individuals with higher-level degrees were more likely to make food purchases at specialty shops (F=3.492; p=0.034). Concerns pertaining to the 'healthiness' of food were significantly different by gender (F=3.107, p=0.081) with women expressing greater interest than men. Older respondents regarded the 'taste' of food to be an important determinant of quality (F=4.833; p<0.001). Respondents with a graduate degree expressed purchasing more organic products than respondents with undergraduate or high school degrees (F=2.593; p=0.079). This relationship did not appear different by income group.

Using Pearson's correlations to initially assess the relationship between independent variables (socioeconomics, attitudes, information seeking /knowledge, habits, and context) and the dependent variable (shopping at specialty stores for novelty food items), as measured using elements of the FRL instrument, we determined bi-directional relationship between the variables.

Attitudes were strongly positively correlated with information seeking (r=.577, p<.0001) and context (r=.432, p<.0001) as indicated in the Zepeda and Deal (2009) overview of alphabet theory. However, habits were not correlated strongly with either context or attitudes. Similarly, standardized socioeconomic variables (gender, age, income, education, and household) were only related to habits (age: r=-.261, p=.006; household: r=.246, p=.009). Behaviors were strongly correlated with attitudes (r=.629, p<.001), information seeking (r=.361, p<.001), context (r=.482, p<.001), and education level (r=.237, p=.012). Using logically forced directionality (i.e., attitudes being influenced by context) a strong path analysis model was developed (Figure 3). Model fit indices are: Chi-square=54.974 (d.f.=3, p<.0001); RMSR=0.0; AIC=16.0. The model reveals that changing attitudes through information/knowledge and context can alter consumer behaviors.

Figure 3. Results of path analysis of standardized variables and force uni-directional relationships revealing factors influencing the purchase of specialty food products by U.S. consumers

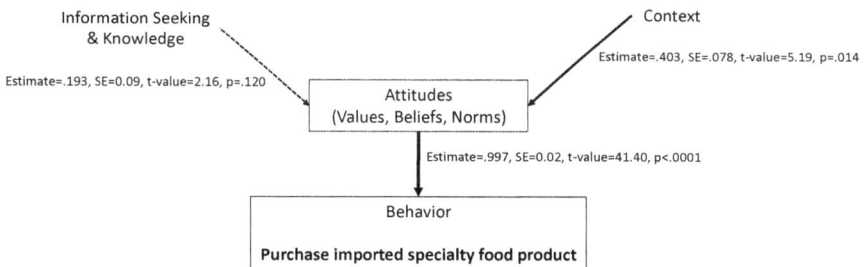

Information Seeking & Knowledge

Context

Estimate=.193, SE=0.09, t-value=2.16, p=.120

Estimate=.403, SE=.078, t-value=5.19, p=.014

Attitudes
(Values, Beliefs, Norms)

Estimate=.997, SE=0.02, t-value=41.40, p<.0001

Behavior

Purchase imported specialty food product

The survey contained three labels developed for Marianna's Vineleaves *ntolmadakia*, taking into account design characteristics unique to 'high-end' and 'artisanal' products. The second label, a combination of 'high-end' and 'artisanal' design characteristics with neutral tones (not a transparent label), easy to read fonts, abstract and modern imagery, and the inclusion of marketing terms deemed important for U.S. consumers (i.e., "Mediterranean" and "healthy") was preferred by the majority (64.3 percent) of respondents. Preferences for the three unique labels for Marianna's did not differ by socioeconomics. Preference for the three labels did vary by FRL clusters, although the majority in each cluster preferred Label 2. Lack of variation in preference for labels may have resulted from a lack of variation in the design of the labels. The first label was described by a respondent to have a "smooth and slick [design], very confined, [which] highlights the brand name and keeps everything else small." Respondents may not have ranked this label to be their favorite because they also described it to be "very hard to read." Label 2 was described as "colorful, visually appealing, vivid."

Many respondents noted that they preferred Label 2 because "the contrast of color [made it] easy to read." A respondent also mentioned that the "font type and size matters." Respondents emphasized that Labels 2 and 3 were very similar. One respondent stated that they "liked the swirls on #3, but prefer the color of #2." Another wrote, "[the] colors in #3 are more subtle, the spiral set off the actual name of the product." One respondent expressed that "green makes [them] think of natural or organic food" when indicating why they preferred Label 3.

5.   DISCUSSION

With more U.S. consumers interested in the Mediterranean diet, small-scale producers in Greece and the Mediterranean region have an opportunity to expand their markets. Food marketing literature assessing consumer segments in the form of food-related lifestyles, socioeconomics, attitudes, values, context, or combinations thereof, suggests that specialty food consumers can be identified and strategies can be employed to market products to these customers. For example, the FRL adventurous and rational food consumer segments have been recognized as the two key segments interested in purchasing and consuming specialty food products. These consumer segments are driven by health, quality, taste, freshness and value for money. Packaging aesthetics can be altered to target these consumer clusters. For example, the adventurous consumer seeks new products advertised by exotic packaging.

Our data revealed that U.S. consumers hold existing attitudes towards Mediterranean foods, a genre in which food produced in Greece is included. Free listing, taste tests, and focus group discussions revealed that Mediterranean food is considered healthy, fresh, and tasty. Analyses of descriptions of Greek products already available in the U.S. market revealed that producers either have had a hand in generating these attitudes, or draw on the attitudes when marketing their products. Product descriptions frequently contained the terms 'healthy' and 'fresh.' Pile sort analyses revealed that packaging aesthetics such as glass jars, label and font colors, font size and style, and image and word arrangement influence how U.S. consumers perceive a product. High-end products, which consumers are willing to pay more for, are sold in glass jars, with transparent labels, easy to read large font, and a minimalist design. Artisanal, imported products have similar characteristics, but include modern graphics, twine around the lid, and sometimes a tag providing additional surface area to describe the product or the producer more completely.

Our survey findings revealed what, if any, consumer characteristics (1) motivated specialty food consumption, and (2) preferences for specialty food product packaging. While we hypothesized that certain FRL clusters would be drawn to different product labels, we found no variation in label preference. Label preferences also did not vary by socioeconomics. This may have been due to the lack of variation in the product labels, but may also be an indication of the small sample size and lack of variation in the FRL clusters within the sample. Using the FRL instrument to assess what factors motivate specialty food consumption, we found that, as the alphabet theory suggests, attitudes, context, and information seeking all influence behavior. Forcing logical, unidirectional relationships, path analysis reveals that providing information to consumers about a specific product (or food genera, such as Mediterranean), influences attitudes, which drive behaviors. In addition, placing consumers in certain context (social events specifically tied to a regional diet) can also influence attitudes and subsequently behaviors. While producers may not be able to alter context directly, information about the product and the producer can be conveyed through multiple avenues included on labels, producer websites, and sampling events. Product labels can offer serving suggestions, or integration of a product into theme related meals or events as a way to indirectly alter the context within which the product is consumed. Our analysis did not indicate that habit formation mediated the relationship between attitudes, context, and behavior as suggested by Zepeda and Deal (2009). This may be because our measurements for habits was not sensitive enough, or our sample size too small to reveal the strength of the relationship.

Collectively these findings suggest the small-scale producers should make efforts through their product packaging, but also through other media outlets such as webpages, to inform and educate consumers. In the case of Marianna's Vineleaves, for example, the business has established a strong reputation among consumers in northern Greece. The product is recognized and valued for its quality, and has received many accolades from the food industry. An initial step towards successful entry into the U.S. market is transferring the knowledge of this reputation to U.S. consumers. Marianna's Vineleaves might consider developing a website that directly communicates with the U.S. consumer. The website might contain a narrative of the family and company history to provide the uninformed consumer with details about how the products were initially developed, the level of quality that should be expected from the product, and the highly regarded nature of the business in Greece.

6. CONCLUSION

This study used a mixed method approach to identify factors that influence U.S. consumer preferences for specialty imported food products and identifies successful marketing strategies. Through a free listing exercise, particular words were identified that are associated with Greek food by the U.S. consumer. These words were found to be commonly used by current specialty food producers to market *ntolmadakia* in the U.S. A taste testing involving unlabeled samples of *ntolmadakia* was executed to gain insight on U.S consumer preferences towards these products. Survey results revealed that producers should seek to provide consumers with information about their products and businesses in order to shift attitudes and drive behaviors. Findings of the study are limited as data were collected from a relatively small, homogenous sample living within a narrow geographical setting. Consequently, participants cannot be considered representative of the U.S., and as such, results from this study must be taken with caution. Further research should be conducted among a larger and more diverse U.S. consumer group to determine if the consumer preferences identified in this study are generalizable. Even so, the approach we used to investigate how small-scale artisanal food products are perceived by the U.S. market can guide other organizations in their efforts to expand to new international consumer markets.

7.   ACKNOWLEDGEMENT

We would like to thank the family and employees of Marianna's Vineleaves, and in particular, Sakis Kazakis, for his inspiration, guidance, patience, and time.

REFERENCES

Bernard, H.R., 2006. Research Methods in Anthropology: Qualitative and Quantitative Approaches, Fourth Edition. Rowman and Littlefield, New York, USA.

Brunsø, K., and Grunert, K.G., 1995. Development and testing of a cross-culturally valid instrument: Food-related lifestyle. Advances in Consumer Research, Vol. 22, pp. 475-480.

Brunsø, K., and Grunert, K.G., 1998. Cross-cultural similarities and differences in shopping for food. Journal of Business Research, Vol. 42, pp. 145-150.

Cannon, J., 2005. Notions of region and the Mediterranean diet in food advertising: Quality marks or subjective criteria? British Food Journal, Vol. 107, No. 2, pp. 74-83.

Cronbach, L.J., 1951. Coefficient alpha and the internal structure of tests. Psychometric, Vol. 16, No. 3, pp. 297-334.

DataMonitor, 2005. Developing Products with a Price Premium. Capitalizing on consumers' growing tendencies to trade-up. DataMonitor, London, UK.

Demby, E., 1974. "Psychographics and from Whence It Came." In William D. Wells (ed.), Lifestyle and Psychographics (pp. 11-30). American Marketing Association, Chicago, USA.

Gravlee, C., 1998. The Uses and Limitations of Free Listing in Ethnographic Research. Retrieved from http://nersp.osg.ufl.edu/~ufruss/cognitive/DOCUMENTS/freelists.htm.

Herr, P.M., 1989. Priming price: Prior knowledge and context effects. Journal of consumer research, Vol 16, pp. 67-75.

Kline, R., 2005. Principles and practice of structural equation modeling. Guildford Press, New York, USA.

Lai, A., 1991. Consumption situation and product knowledge in the adoption of a new product. European Journal of Marketing, Vol. 25, No. 10, pp. 55-67.

Lappalainen, R., Kearney, J., and Gibney, M., 1998. A pan EU survey of consumer attitudes to food, nutrition and health: an overview. Food quality and preference, Vol. 9, No. 6, pp. 467-478.

Lone, K., and Bech, B., 2001. "Food-Related Lifestyle: A Segmentation Approach to European Food Consumers." In L.J. Frewer, et al. (eds.), Food, People and Society: A European Perspective of Consumers' Food Choices. Springer-Verlag, Berlin, Germany.

Nie, C., & Zepeda, L., 2011. Lifestyle segmentation of US food shoppers to examine organic and local food consumption. Appetite, Vol. 57, No. 1, pp. 28-37.

Northup, T., 2014. Truth, lies, and packaging: How food marketing creates a false sense of health. Food Studies, Vol. 3, No. 1, pp. 9-18.

Organization for Economic Co-operation and Development, 2014. Society at a glance 2014, Highlights Greece - The crisis and its aftermath. Retrieved from https://www.oecd.org/greece/OECD-SocietyAtaGlance2014-Highlights-Greece.pdf.

O'Sullivan, C., Scholderer, J., and Cowan, C., 2005. Measurement equivalence of the food related lifestyle instrument (FRL) in Ireland and Great Britain. Food Quality and Preference, Vol. 16, pp. 1–12.

Purcell, D., 2015. Today's Specialty Food Consumer, 2015. Specialty Food Association, New York, USA. Retrieved from https://www.specialtyfood.com/media/filer_public/37/76/3776e618-8a5f-477b-a7a7-9f373814bf96/consumerreport2015_8pgs.pdf.

Rong-Da Liang, A., and Lim, W. M., 2011. Exploring the online buying behavior of specialty food shoppers. International Journal of Hospitality Management, Vol. 30, No. 4, pp. 855-865.

Scholderer, J., Brunsø, K., Bredahl, L., and Grunert, K.G., 2004. Cross-cultural validity of the food-related lifestyles instrument (FRL) within Western Europe. Appetite, Vol. 42, No. 2, pp. 197-211.

Silayoi, P., and Speece, M., 2004. Packaging and purchase decisions: An exploratory study on the impact of involvement level and time pressure. British Food Journal, Vol. 106, No. 8, pp. 607-628.

Silayoi, P., and Speece, M., 2007. The importance of packaging attributes: A conjoint analysis approach. European Journal of Marketing, Vol. 41, No. 11/12, pp. 1495-1517.

Steptoe, A., Pollard, T. M., and Wardle, J., 1995. Development of a measure of the motives underlying the selection of food: The food choice questionnaire. Appetite, Vol. 25, No. 3, pp. 267-284.

Wang, E., 2013. The influence of visual packaging design on perceived food product quality, value, and brand preference. International Journal of Retail & Distribution Management, Vol. 41, No. 10, pp. 805-816.

Tepper, B.J., Choi, Y.S., and Nayga, R.M., 1997. Understanding food choice in adult men: influence of nutrition knowledge, food beliefs and dietary restraint. Food Quality and Preference, Vol. 8, No. 4, pp. 307-317.

Vignali-Ryding, D., Sanchez, J.D., and Vignali, G., 2003. The delicatessen & specialty food market in the Northwest. British Food Journal, Vol. 105, No. 8, pp. 551–558.

Weller, S.C., and Romney, A.K., 1988. Systematic Data Collection: Qualitative Research Methods Series 10. Sage, Thousand Oaks, USA.

Wells, W.D., 1975. Psychographics: A critical review. Journal of Marketing Research, Vol. 12, pp. 196-213.

Wile, R., 2015. The Real Reason Why Young People Are Snacking More. Retrieved from http://fusion.net/story/164423/survey-more-young- people-are-snacking-to-kill-their-emotions/

Wycherley, A., McCarthy, M., and Cowan, C., 2008. Specialty food orientation of food related lifestyle (FRL) segments in Great Britain. Food Quality and Preference, Vol. 19, No. 5, pp. 498-510.

Zepeda, L., and Deal, D., 2009. Organic and local food consumer behavior: Alphabet theory. International Journal of Consumer Studies, Vol. 33, No. 6, pp. 697-705.

Chapter 5

GREEK OLIVE OIL IN THE UK: EVIDENCE ON THE PERCEPTION OF LOCAL IMPORTERS ON PRODUCT CHARACTERISTICS

Christos Soulios, Athanasios Bizmpiroulas[1]
and Konstantinos Rotsios

Perrotis College, Marinou Antipa 54, Thessaloniki, 55102, Greece

ABSTRACT

The agri-food sector has traditionally been one of the most important ones for the Greek economy. It accounts for one third of the country's total exports with an established strong presence in the European countries and an increasing trend in the US. The country produces 20% of the world's total olive oil production, 75% of which is of premium quality "extra-virgin". In 2015, the product ranked fourth among the top exported products of Greece. Currently, the UK market is the seventh largest market for Greek products, the total value of which reaches approximately one billion euro per year. This paper focuses on the perceptions of Greek olive oil importers in the UK. It examines their perceptions on the characteristics and attributes olive oil consumers in the UK value the most.

Seven in depth interviews were conducted with Chief Executive Officers (CEOs) of importing firms since they have a holistic view of the market specific conditions and consumer demands in their capacity as intermediaries between the producers and the end consumers. Through the interviews, the product's organoleptic characteristics (taste, aroma, color) and attributes such as price, packaging and certifications of Greek olive oil are identified and ranked by importance. To the best of our knowledge and despite its potential, the UK olive oil market has never been examined before.

---

[1]abizbi@afs.edu.gr

The findings are presented and analyzed, and their practical implications are discussed. Finally, the limitations of this paper are identified and topics for further research are suggested.

KEYWORDS

Olive Oil, Greek, UK, Exports, Imports.

JEL CLASSIFICATION CODES

F14

1. INTRODUCTION

Greece is the third largest olive oil producer in the world, following Spain and Italy (International Olive Council, 2015). The total production is approximately 400,000 tons/year, 75% of which is of premium quality "extra virgin" (Enterprise Greece, 2008). The main olive oil producing regions are the island of Crete and the region of Kalamata in the Peloponnese (appr. 65% of the county's total production). The most common variety is the "Koroneiki", which is also the most well-known in international markets (Roubos, Moustakas & Aravanopoulos, 2010). Olive oil ranked fourth among all Greek exports in 2015 and approximately 90% is exported to the European Union. Roughly 80% is sold in bulk and 20% is bottled and marketed under various Greek brands. This research focuses on the UK market, as it is considered a high potential market for Greek olive oil. In 2013, the United Kingdom (UK) imported 1,473 tons of Greek olive oil (Bettini, 2014). Overall, oil olive consumption in the UK has been rising the last years and the country ranks 10th in per capita consumption of olive oil; thus, it is not a mature market in terms of olive oil consumption. Additionally, the country has a high per capita income (Noble, 2014). Furthermore, UK consumers following the scandals concerning poor quality olive oil which was impure (a mixture of 80% sunflower and 20% olive oil) started to be more cautious when purchasing olive oil (Henley, 2012). The aim of this research paper is to investigate the perception of UK importers on Greek olive oil in regards to the desired organoleptic characteristics and aspects such as the price, the packaging, the quality assurance and to provide olive oil exporters with a better understanding of the UK market needs.

2. LITERATURE REVIEW

Olive oil

According to the International Olive Council olive oil (nd) is:" Virgin olive oils are the oils obtained from the fruit of the olive tree (Olea europaea L.) solely by mechanical or other physical means under conditions, particularly thermal, that do not lead to alterations in the oil, and which have not undergone any treatment other than washing, decantation, centrifugation and filtration". All olive tree varieties can be used for the production of olive oil however they have different characteristics, such as the acidity levels, the portion on grams of oleic acid per 100 grams of olive oil, the aroma, the taste and finally, the color (Pouliarekou et al., 2011).

Consumer behavior and olive oil purchasing criteria

According to Espejel et al. (2007) the most effective way to predict consumers' behavior is to identify their intentions. In order to fully understand consumer behavior, aspects like attitudes, preferences and motivations must be considered. Thus, the purchasing intention is a future indication for the consumers' behavior, which can help to identify their consuming patterns. Moreover, attitudes are the outcome of the a) cognitive, b) emotions and c) projected consumer actions. Attitudes can be influenced by parameters like family, information or experience and can predict consumer purchasing patterns in the near future.

Consumer behavior comprises of many elements, since it examines the processes that take place when individuals or groups choose, purchase and use or decline to use products or services in order to fulfill their needs. Moreover, Solomon, Russell-Bennett & Previte (2013) categorize consumers based on a) their age, gender, income and profession (descriptive &demographics characteristics) and b) their lifestyle, status, interests in clothing or music and personality (the psychographic criteria). According to Mili (2006), many changes have occurred in regards to food buying decisions and consumption patterns. In developed countries, consumers mainly purchase food differentiated based on its intrinsic and extrinsic characteristics. The buying decisions are influenced by perceptions, preferences, values and other emotions rather than price or income, thus those who care most about their health, the variety, the safety and the quality of the product or service are not dissuaded by price. Taking into consideration the above expectations, olive oil satisfies consumers due to its health properties and its gastronomic abilities.

Education and income are very important decision making factors, especially in regards to food purchases. Consumers with higher educational and income levels are more health conscious, purchase healthy foods more often and are willing to pay premium prices (Bere et al., 2008). In recent years, an increasing number of consumers have been educated through TV cooking shows, media and state campaigns about the health benefits of olive oil consumption and as a result its consumption has increased. Today's consumers have a better understanding and the skills required to identify good quality olive oil (Garcia-Gonzalez & Aparicio, 2010). However, consumer awareness in regards to the products uses (cook daily, not only for "special" occasions) remains crucial.

As Guinard & Santosa (2010) note, products can be classified into two categories: the "think" and the "feel" products. The "think" products are purchased for their functional use and the decision is based on the value for money criterion, while the "feel" products are purchased to fulfill emotional desires. Olive oil can be purchased as a "think" product for cooking to enhance food taste and for its health benefits as well as a "feel" product when used for special occasions.

Several olive oil characteristics that influence its selection have been identified in literature. More specifically some studies have examined the role of the intrinsic characteristics, such as taste, aroma, color, while others focused on extrinsic characteristics such as the package, the label etc. (Imani et al., 2013). According to Krystallis & Ness (2005), the most significant criteria for purchasing olive oil are the quality certifications, the country of origin, the package size, the color, the label, the brand name and the price. As Aprile et al. (2012) state consumers prefer to purchase olive oil with a "strong" country brand name, (e.g. Greece, Italy and Spain), because it indicates quality. Quality certifications are also important and influence the consumers' buying decision because they provide a sense of safety. Furthermore, consumers are willing to pay premium prices for certified products, so quality certifications affect price too (Chan-Halbrendt et al., 2010). Regarding bottle size consumers prefer bottles between 500-750 ml since they can be easily stored. The brand name also affects the consumer's decision due to the relationship between the brand and the product's quality (McCluskey & Loureiro, 2003). Color and label are some of the least important criteria consumers take into consideration in order to purchase olive oil (Dekhili et al., 2011).

Consumers in different countries appear to have diverse criteria for purchasing olive oil. For instance, Tunisian and French consumers consider taste to be the most important criterion, while packaging is the least important one (Dekhili et al., 2011). On the contrary, for UK consumers packaging and package size are the most important (Garcia et al., 2002). Thus, the consumers' different purchasing criteria in specific markets must be considered before entering a market. Consumers have two dichotomous perceptions in regards to the uses of the product. Olive oil with a "milder flavor" is considered appropriate for cooking while olive oil with a "stronger flavor" for non-cooking uses. The "non-cooking" olive oil can be used as a gift, souvenir, salad dressing or bread dipping (Santosa et al., 2010). Delgado & Guinard (2010) found that mainly women purchase olive oil while the age of the "average" consumers is over thirty years. In regards to their demographic characteristics, their educational and income level was medium to high and the majority of them were single.

3. METHODOLOGY

In order to obtain a better and more detailed understanding of the UK olive oil market, the qualitative approach was chosen and semi structured interviews were utilized. According to DiCicco-Bloom & Carbtree (2006) "Semi-structured interviews are often the sole data source for a qualitative research project and are usually scheduled in advance at a designated time and location outside of everyday events". Due to the use of the semi-structured questions the conversations were structured however respondents had the opportunity to express themselves freely and in an open manner (Whiting, 2008). In addition to the interview questions, probing questions were asked during the interview, in order to clarify the answers or to give more details and information and to extort more data (Changing Minds, nd). The semi structured questionnaire was designed based on literature findings and forwarded to importers in order to verify its clarity and coherence. Following their feedback, the necessary amendments were made. The interviews were audio recorded with the participants' permission for transcription. This gave the opportunity for smooth and fast flow interviews and a verbatim transcription. The respondents' anonymity was guaranteed to ensure sincere and meaningful answers. The interviews were conducted separately, semi-structured questions were used, and the answers were recorded and transcripted to allow for a more systematic and accurate analysis (Aluwihare-Samaranayake, 2012).

The sample consisted only of Greek olive oil importers in order to increase the practical value of this research. Since they act as mediators between the producers and the final consumers they have to be aware of the needs and wants of the consumers, in order to import the appropriate products. The fact that they are in the middle of the demand and supply chain makes them "experts" in their field (Alvarez et al., 2011). So, aspects like credibility, dependability and confirmability which are regarded as important for the qualitative analysis were fulfilled (Baxter & Jack, 2008).

The respondents were identified after an internet search and with the assistance of the Greek International Business Association (SEVE). They were asked to participate in this research by e-mail and seven professional Greek olive oil importers in UK agreed to. All of them are Chief Executive Officers (CEO's) and had a full insight of their companies, the sales of the Greek olive oil and of the market specific conditions. Various olive oil characteristics, such as taste, aroma and their importance for the UK consumers were examined. Additionally, parameters, such as the price, olive oil variety, country of origin, and brand, were analyzed. Finally, the UK consumers' awareness of the most well-known Greek olive oil producing regions was explored in order to determine their influence on the purchasing decision process. This analysis reveals the characteristics of Greek olive oil required to successfully compete in the UK market.

Table 1: Respondents' characteristics

Interviewee #	Position	Experience	Number of employees
I#1	Chief executive officer	4	3
I#2	Chief executive officer	2	5
I#3	Chief executive officer	4	25
I#4	Chief executive officer	3	2
I#5	Chief executive officer	19	7
I#6	Chief executive officer	18	1
I#7	Chief executive officer	1	1

4. ANALYSIS AND DISCUSSION

To the best of our knowledge, this is the first study on olive oil characteristics UK consumers value most when purchasing the product. The characteristics that influence the consumers' buying behavior in regards to olive oil, are the country of origin (Newaz et al., 2012), the price (Dekhili & D' Hauteville, 2009), the packaging (Garcia et al., 2002) and the quality certifications (Chan-Halbrendt et al., 2010). The objective of this research is to identify the perception of Greek olive oil importers on these characteristics and to determine their significance in the UK market. These characteristics are depicted in Table 1.

Experience

According to Stoian et al. (2011) entrepreneurs who live or use to live in the same country their enterprise operates or have studied in this country, have a better perception of the local market and the market specific conditions. Additionally, a firm's experience is measured by its age (years of operation) and its experience in international markets. All respondents live and operate in the UK, so they are aware of the local market particularities. Furthermore, they all started importing Greek products since the establishment of their businesses. There is a variety among the sample's firms in regards to the years of operation (Table 1). Most of the companies operate for more than three years which is considered a reasonable period of operational experience. Only two, I#2 and I#7, have less than three years of experience, two and one year respectively. As noted earlier they all are CEO's in their companies and have holistic view of the specific market, a fact that further enhances the credibility and the practical implications of this research. According to Robst (2007) educated individuals have different skills and will most probably change occupation more often than the ones with fewer skills. In our sample, four out of the seven respondents, had different careers before their current occupation. Although they have different educational backgrounds, they realized the potential of Greek food products in the UK market and started to import. As I#1 said: "I was looking for a more satisfying job/occupation; I wanted to start something of my own. As I have been in London for twenty years, I have a good understanding of the Greek food products' potential in the UK market, and I thought it would be a good opportunity."

Firm's size

In today's economic and business environment, larger companies have the required human and financial resources and as a result they have better changes to be competitive. More specifically, due their resources, competencies and knowhow they face a lower risk of failure in foreign market, and can take advantage of economies of scale (Gourio & Roys, 2014). However, as Stoian et al. (2011) state, the firm's size is no longer a key success factor; employee commitment is. In Europe, companies with less than two hundred fifty employees are considered as SME. More specifically, enterprises with less than ten employees are considered to be "micro", with less than fifty "small" and with less than two hundred and fifty employees "medium" (European Commission, 2014). Almost all firms in the sample are micro enterprises, as depicted in Table. The largest number of employees is twenty-five. Additionally, respondents I#6 and I#7 run the business alone. According to Tomiura (2006) size is not as an important as the productivity of the firm is. Considering the firms' age, I#6 has eighteen years of experience and noted that "I am proud of my business", while I#7 operates as start-up enterprise. Despite the fact that there is only one person working in the company (#6), the eighteen years of operation show market experience so it can be considered as a credible source. On the contrary, I#7, has little experience in operating the business. However, this allows for a comparison of the responses with the other more "experienced" firms in the sample.

Supplier characteristics

The desired characteristics of the Greek exporting firms were also examined in this research. Table 2 bellow summarizes the responses of the UK importers. I#4 did not identify any characteristic, as they have a vertical integration production system; they produce, package and sell their own olive oil. The main characteristic most importers (three out of six) require from their business partners is quality. "The only thing I care about is the quality of the olive oil" states I#3. The next most desired characteristics are prompt and accurate communication between the suppliers and the importers and product certifications. Both I#1 and I#2 mentioned that prompt and clear communication is an important characteristic. As I#2 noted, "Especially for the Greek firms, due to the country's current situation, communication is very important". Certifications are important in order to explicate the quality and safety of the olive oil in the UK market. Numerous agencies check the quality of the olive oil, the label and the accuracy of the information on it; as I#7 mentioned "Certifications are very important in order to enter into the UK market". Furthermore, respondents I#1 and I#6 note that there is an increasing demand for infused olive oil.

Table 1: Characteristics required from the suppliers

Interviewee	I#1	I#2	I#3	I#4	I#5	I#6	I#7
Communication	✓	✓					
Quality (product & producer)	✓		✓				✓
Experience	✓						
Organized units		✓					
Punctuality		✓					
Certifications		✓					✓
Trust					✓		
Honest						✓	
Price							✓
Packaging	✓				✓		

Important olive oil characteristics for the UK market

This first question examines the general olive oil characteristics required and not specifically for the Greek olive oil. As depicted in Table 3, respondents provided different answers in regards to the essential characteristics. Taste has been identified as the most important characteristic that influences the consumers' buying decision; aroma is second followed by price and country of origin. Interestingly, the least important characteristics are packaging, the variety and the certifications. The majority of the respondents believe that the organoleptic characteristics are the most important ones. However, as I#5 stated: "Certifications are the most important", I#5. On the other hand, I#2 mentioned that price is the most important criterion to import olive oil in the UK, while according to I#6 "If taste is good, consumers will be willing to pay a premium price for olive oil".

Table 2: Characteristics of imported olive oil in the UK

Interviewee	I#1	I#2	I#3	I#4	I#5	I#6	I#7
Taste	✓		✓	✓		✓	✓
Aroma	✓		✓				✓
Price	✓	✓					
Country of origin		✓					✓
Packaging		✓					
Variety			✓				
Certifications					✓		

Important characteristics for Greek olive oil imports in the UK market

There are different opinions among the respondents concerning the criteria UK consumers have for purchasing Greek olive oil. According to I#6 because the product is packaged in clear glass bottles, color is the most important criterion, whereas, I#1 believes olive oils sold in supermarkets cannot differentiate significantly, since they all appear the same on the shelves and it is not possible for consumers to distinguish the products from each other in regards to their taste or aroma. Respondent I#1 gives consumers the opportunity to taste various types of olive oil in order to purchase the one that best satisfies their personal preferences. As he notes, "For our customers, the most important criteria are taste and aroma. We give them the opportunity to taste the olive oil before they decide to purchase it. We want them to become aware and to understand the real differences between olive oils and not to purchase the product just for its package". The most important criterion for UK consumers is taste, while certifications are the least important. Packaging is the second most important one, followed by the color and the region. Surprisingly, among the least important criteria are the aroma, the price and the health benefits of olive oil A past research by Garcia et al. (2002) has showed that, packaging and the size of the package were the most important purchasing criteria for UK olive oil consumers. This change may be explained by the fact that more consumers became aware of the product's uses the last years.

Table 3: Criteria for UK consumers to purchase Greek olive oil

Interviewee	Taste	Aroma	Brand packaging	Region	Health benefits	Price	Color	Certification -Awards
I#1	✓	✓	✓	✓				✓
I#2			✓	✓	✓	✓		
I#3	✓						✓	
I#4	✓							
I#5	✓					✓		
I#6			✓				✓	
I#7	✓	✓	✓	✓	✓		✓	

Olive oil producing regions

In regards to the most well-known Greek olive oil producing region, results are quite puzzling. Most respondents initially replied that Crete is the most well-known producing region in the country, but on a second thought, they identified Kalamata as the most famous one. More specifically, four of the respondents identified Crete as the most well know region, while six mentioned Kalamata (two respondents, ranked it as the first most well-known region and four as the second. Lastly, two of the respondents named Lakonia as well-known olive oil producing region in Greece.

Table 4: Most well-known Greek olive oil producing regions

Interviewee	Crete	Kalamata	Laconia
I#1	✓	✓	✓
I#2		✓	
I#3			✓
I#4	✓	✓	
I#5		✓	
I#6	✓	✓	
I#7	✓	✓	

A possible explanation for the above results is that Crete is one of the most popular summer vacation destinations for UK tourists and according to Kavallari et al. (2011) tourism is the best direct marketing strategy. The numerous tourists that visit Crete, taste its olive oil and are seeking for it in the UK. On the other hand, Kalamata is a well-known region for its edible (table) olives a fact that also boosts the region's image and reputation in regards to olive oil. According to I#2, UK consumers often confuse olive oil and edible (table) olives produced in Kalamata and ask for olive oil from this region. As I#5 stated "British consumers believe that the top quality Greek olive oil is produced in Kalamata because the region is well known for the production of the finest table olives".

The importance of price and price determinants

According to Krystallis and Ness (2005) price is one of the most important factors affecting consumer behavior and the buying decision process. Price can be affected by many factors such as the material, the shape, the color, the size of the package, the country of origin and variety. Five of the respondents provided answers concerning the price; the average selling price directly to the final consumer or to specialty stores, but not to supermarkets, is ten Euros/liter for the top quality, "extra virgin" olive oil. The major selling points are delicatessen stores, e-shops or other food stores. The price of the olive oil sold in supermarkets is very low, however the quality is questionable. As I#5 noted, "Supermarkets sell olive oil at a lower price than I pay my supplier". The majority of the respondents buy olive oil at the market price, with the exception of I#6 who pays two or three times the current market price in order to buy the finest quality. As he stated "I am willing to pay much more to buy good quality olive oil".

Table 5: Parameters affecting price

Interviewee	Organoleptic characteristics	Packaging	Country of origin	Protected Designation of Origin PDO	Variety	Brand	Retailer	Quality
I#1	✓			✓				
I#2	✓	✓		✓				
I#3					✓			✓
I#4	✓	✓	✓					
I#5		✓				✓	✓	
I#6		✓	✓					
I#7	✓		✓					✓

The most important factors that affect olive oil price in the UK, are shown in Table 6. First are the product's organoleptic characteristics such as taste, aroma, color and packaging. The second most important characteristic is the country of origin, followed the PDO certification. According to the respondents, the PDO sign "guarantees" the quality of the olive oil, because the whole production process, from raw material to the finished product takes place under very strict and specific rules and standards. The least important price affecting parameters, according to the importers' perception are the variety, the brand name, the retailer and the quality of the product. It is important to note that only two of the seven respondents identified quality as an important price determinant for olive oil.

Consumption of olive oil in the UK

According to the respondents, the main use of olive oil in the UK is for salad dressing. The percentage of consumers that use it for cooking remains very small, but it is increasing. Lastly, they noted that currently only luxury restaurants use olive oil for salad dressing and for cooking.

The majority of the respondents believe that olive oil is steadily becoming an important ingredient of the UK diet, as the consumers' awareness in regards to the health benefits and the uses of the product has increased. According to I#5, rapeseed olive has a bigger market share and consumers use it because of its lower price. However, I#1 believes that the changing eating habits of the UK consumers lead to an increase of olive oil consumption. Krystallis & Ness (2005) argue that consumers in northern European countries such as the UK, are not fully aware of the various food producing processes and have little knowledge about their health benefits. Currently, the increasing number of UK consumers using olive oil, facilitates the diffusion of the Mediterranean's diet principles among consumers in this market. With the exception of I#3 and I#5, the rest of the respondents believe that Mediterranean diet in the UK has become more popular, mostly among high educated individuals and an increasing number of consumers adopt its principles.

Segments of olive oil consumers

In regards to olive oil consumers, the respondents' common point of view is that they are educated individuals who belong to the middle or upper class. In particular, I#1 believes that individuals who consume olive oil, belong to the middle and upper class, enjoy to travel and have tasted olive oil in their journeys. Furthermore, I#2 has identified two target groups that consume olive oil, a) the foreigners living in the UK who come from olive oil producing countries, and b) the locals who are passionate about healthy living. Similarly, I#4 believes that people with higher education, who are aware of the product's health benefits, are willing to pay a premium price for it. I#6 argues that higher income individuals and a healthy eating lifestyle, consume more olive oil than lower income individuals. Finally, I#4 mentioned the difference between Greek consumers, who despite their socio-economic status consume large quantities of olive and the UK ones who consume much smaller quantities.

5.   CONCLUSION AND RECOMMENDATIONS

The aim of this research paper is to examine the perception of the Greek olive oil importers in the UK, on the product's characteristics in order to successfully compete in this market. To the best of our knowledge most of the literature, with the exception of Garcia et al. (2002), examines the characteristics of the olive oil in mature markets, not in developing ones like the UK. Furthermore, prior literature focuses on the consumers' perception and not on the importers'. However, importers are the link between the exporters and the markets and can provide meaningful insights on the matter.

The qualitative approach was used in order to gain an in depth understanding of the importers' perception. Data was gathered with the use of semi structured interviews which allows for a broader analysis and discussion. All the respondents were the CEOs in their companies, a position that enables them to have a holistic view of the business operations and of the specific market. The main limitation of this research is the sample's small size; the researchers did not have direct access to more importing firms in the UK.

In regards to product characteristics, parameters such as the criteria for importing olive oil in the UK, the awareness of the olive oil producing regions in addition to the factors that the price of the olive oil in the UK were examined. Taste was identified as the most important criterion for purchasing olive oil in the

UK. Aroma was the second most important criterion for olive oil in general, whereas in the case of Greek olive oil the brand and packaging ranked in the second place. Garcia et al. (2002) examined the consumers of olive oil in the UK market and indicated as the most important criterion packaging and the size of the bottle. On the contrary, according to the results of this study, the most important criterion is taste. This finding is an indication that consumers' preferences and purchasing criteria change, especially when they become aware of the health benefits and different uses of the product.

An interesting finding is that the overall quality of olive oil does not seem to have an impact on its price according to the majority of the respondents. Furthermore, there is confusion among olive oil consumers in the UK in regards to olive oil and edible (table) olives and the region of production. They believe that region of Kalamata is a producer of high quality olive oil because it produces premium quality table olives. Thus, it will be interesting in the future to further explore and clarify the influence of olive oil quality on price and to examine the impact of the "origin" (producing area) on consumer's buying decisions.

To summarize, the respondents' main recommendation for Greek firms is to improve the efficiency of their marketing strategies, since they consider it to be a major weakness. Furthermore, the fact that the second most important criterion of purchasing Greek olive oil is packaging demonstrates the lack of efficient marketing activities. The findings of this study provide useful information to Greek olive oil exporters, as they provide information on the UK olive oil market and specific recommendations to increase their competitiveness in that market.

REFERENCES

Aluwihare-Samaranayake, D 2012, 'Ethics in Qualitative Research: A View of the Participants' and Researchers' World from a Critical Standpoint', International Journal Of Qualitative Methods, vol.11, no. 2, pp. 64-81

Alvarez, M, Chanda, R & Smith, R 2011, 'The potential for bi-lateral agreements in medical tourism: A qualitative study of stakeholder perspectives from the UK and India', Globalization and Health, vol. 7, no. 11

Aprile, M C, Caputo, V & Nayga Jr, R M 2012, 'Consumers' valuation of food quality labels: the case of the European geographic indication and organic farming labels, International Journal of Consumer Studies, vol. 36, no. 2, pp. 158-165

Baxter, P & Jack, S 2008, 'Qualitative case study methodology: study design and implementation for novice researchers', The Qualitative Report, vol. 13, no. 4, pp. 544-559

Bere, E, Van Lenthe, F, Klepp, K & Brug, J 2008, 'Why do parents' education level and income affect the amount of fruits and vegetables adolescents eat?', EUPHA, pp. 611-615

Bettini O, 2014, Olive Oil Annual, viewed on 2 May 2015, http://gain.fas.usda.gov/Recent%20GAIN%20Publications/Olive%20Oil%20Annual%202014_Rome_Greece_5-14-2014.pdf

Changing Minds, nd, Probing, viewed on 5 May 2015, http://changingminds.org/techniques/questioning/probing.htm

Chan-Halbrendt, C, Zhllima, E, Sisior, G, Imani, D & Leonetti, L 2010, 'Consumer preference for olive oil in Tirana, Albania', International Food and Agribusiness Management Review, vol. 13, no. 3, pp. 55-74

Dekhili, S & D' Hauteville, F 2009, 'Effect of the region of origin on the perceived quality of olive oil: An experimental approach using a control group', Food Quality and Prefernce, pp. 525-532

Dekhili, S, Sirieix, L & Cohen, E 2011, 'How consumers choose olive oil: the importance of origin cues', Food Quality and Preferences, pp. 757-762

Delgado, C & Guinard, J X 2010, 'How do consumer hedonic ratings for extra virgin olive oil relate to quality ratings by experts and descriptive analysis ratings?', Food Quality and Preferences, pp. 213-225

DiCicco-Bloom, B, & Crabtree, B 2006, 'The qualitative research interview', Medical Education, vol. 40, no. 4, pp. 314-321

Espejel, J, Fandos, C &Flavian, C 2007, 'The role of intrinsic and extrinsic quality attributes on consumer behavior for traditional food products', Managing Service Quality: An International Journal, vol. 17, no. 6, pp. 681-701Espejel, J, Enterprise Greece, 2008, Food & Agriculture, http://www.enterprisegreece.gov.gr/en/investment-sectors/food-&-agriculture

European Commission, 2014, What is an SME?, viewed on 8 May 2015, http://ec.europa.eu/enterprise/policies/sme/facts-figures-analysis/sme-definition/index_en.htm

Garcia, M, Aragones, Z & Poole, N 2002, 'A repositioning strategy for olive oil in the UK market', Agribusiness, vol. 18, no. 2, pp. 163-180

Garcia-Gonzalez, D & Aparicio, R 2010, 'Research in olive oil: challenges for the future', Journal of Agricultural and Food Chemistry Perspective

Gourio, F & Roys, N 2014, 'Size-dependent regulations, firm size distribution, and reallocation', Quantitative Economics, pp. 377- 416

Henley J, 2012, How to tell if your olive oil is the real thing, viewed 8 April 2015, http://www.theguardian.com/lifeandstyle/2012/jan/04/olive-oil-real-thing

Imani, D, Zhllima, E, Canavari, M & Elvina, M 2013, 'Segmenting Albanian consumers according to olive oil quality perception and purchasing habits', AGRICULTURAL ECONOMICS REVIEW, vol. 14, no 1, pp.97-112

International Olive Council 2015, World Olive Oil Figures, http://www.internationaloliveoil.org/estaticos/view/131-world-olive-oil-figures

International Olive Council, nd, Designations and definitions of olive oils, http://www.internationaloliveoil.org/estaticos/view/83-designations-and-definitions-of-olive-oils

Kavallari, A, Maas, S & Schmitz, M 2011, 'Examining the determinants of olive oil demand in non-producing countries: evidence from Germany and the UK', Journal of Food Products Marketing, vol. 17, no. 2-3, pp. 355-372

Krystallis, A & Ness, M 2005, 'Consumer Preferences for Quality Foods from a South European Perspective: A Conjoint Analysis Implementation on Greek Olive Oil', International Food and Agribusiness Management Review, vol. 8, no. 2

Mili, S 2006, 'Olive Oil Marketing in Non-Traditional Markets: Prospects and Strategies', New Medit, vol. 5, no. 1, pp. 27-37

McCluskey, J & Loureiro, M L 2003, 'Consumer preferences and willingness to pay for food labeling: a discussion of empirical studies', Journal of Food Distribution Research, vol. 34, no. 3, pp. 95-102

Mili, S 2006, 'Olive Oil Marketing in Non-Traditional Markets: Prospects and Strategies', New Medit, vol. 5, no. 1, pp. 27-37

Newaz, M, Akareem, H & Faruquee, M 2012, 'Imported versus local products: why and how people respond against different categories?', International Journal of Marketing and Technology, vol. 2, no. 7

Noble W, 2014, On the rise: Olive oil tastings in the UK, viewed on 27 April 2015, http://www.oliveoiltimes.com/olive-oil-basics/olive-oil-tasting-in-the-uk/37926

Pouliarekou, E, Badeka, A, Margari, M, Kontakos, S, Longobardi, F & Kontominas, M 2011, 'Characterization and classification of western Greek olive oils according to cultivar and geographical origin based on volatile compounds', Journal of Chromatography A, pp. 7534-7542

Robst, J 2007, 'Education and job match: the relatedness of college major and work', ScienceDirect, pp. 397-407

Roubos, K, Moustakas, M & Aravanopoulos, F 2010, 'Molecular identification of Greek olive (Olea europaea) cultivars based on microsatellite loci', GMR, vol. 9, no. 3, pp. 1865-1876

Santosa, M, Abdi, H & Guinard, J X 2010, 'A mortified sorting task to investigate consumer perceptions of extra virgin olive oils', Food Quality and Preferences, pp. 881-892

Solomon, M, Russell-Bennett, R & Previte, J 2013, 'Consumer Behavior: buying, having, being', 3rd edition, in Pearson

Stoian, M C, Rialp, A & Rialp, J 2011, 'Export performance under the microscope: a glance through Spanish lenses', International Business Review, pp. 117-135

Tomiura, E 2006, 'Foreign outsourcing, exporting and FDI: a productivity comparison at the firm level', viewed on 8 May 2015

Whiting, LS 2008, 'Semi-structured interviews: guidance for novice researchers', Nursing Standard, vol. 22, no. 23, pp. 35-40

Chapter 6

AN ANALYSIS OF EXPORT BARRIERS PERCEPTIONS BY GREEK YOGURT EXPORTERS

Zacharias Papanikolaou[1], Christos Karelakis[2] and Konstadinos Mattas[3]

[1]*PhD Candidate, Aristotle University of Thessaloniki, School of Agriculture, Department of Agricultural Economics,54124, Thessaloniki, Greece, e-mail: zpapanik@agro.auth.gr*

[2]*Democritus University of Thrace, Department Agricultural Development, Pantazidou 193, 68200, Orestiada, Greece, e-mail: chkarel@agro.duth.gr*

[3]*Aristotle University of Thessaloniki, School of Agriculture, Department of Agricultural Economics, 54124, Thessaloniki, Greece, e-mail: mattas@auth.gr*

ABSTRACT

Business internationalization has been a significant development of the past years, resulting in many opportunities which are vital not only for the economic development and independence of most nation states, but also for the growth, profitability and even survival of most business firms. One of the most exported products in Greece is the Greek yogurt, *which,* in 2007, accounted for just 1% of the US yogurt sales and during the period 2008-2010, sales have grown almost 100% for each year. The international increase in the Greek yogurt demand motivated the recent significant growth in its exports. Still, the international markets constitute a highly competitive field in which the Greek yogurt confronts certain impediments. Accordingly, the present study investigates the barriers that Greek yogurt entrepreneurs face during their export activities. Primary data were collected from a survey of 104 Greek yogurt firms through in-depth interviews (structured questionnaire). The data were analyzed through the application of a series of multivariate methods, namely exploratory factor analysis, confirmatory factor analysis and the non-parametric Friedman test. The results indicate that most firms perceive as the major barriers to export the large input costs on export markets, the strict legislation on export markets, bureaucracy in government agencies, the late payments by distributors, and the lack of capital into foreign markets.

KEYWORDS

Internationalization, barriers, Greek yogurt, Exports

1. INTRODUCTION

The growth of firm globalization that influences the business environment has attracted particular policy focus in the recent years (Pinho and Martins, 2010; Zimmermann and Kattuman, 2007). As a result of the world economy, as well as the focus on improving economic deficit, international business involvement is becoming particularly relevant both in terms of national affluence and for individual organisations (Morgan and Katsikeas, 1997). The globalization of the industrial environment increased the competition and exports of the marketplace general. These issues are the simplest ways of the internationalization of firms (Papalexiou, 2009).

Export market activities may increase profitability help to confront any unemployment problems and improve trade balances (United States International Trade Commission, 2010, Koksal, 2008). Small firms are becoming increasingly international and contribute between 25% and 35% of global exports in industrial activities (Andersson and Florén, 2008). However, there are still many firms in developing countries that do not export despite the fact that exporting has less financial and commercial risk, does not require a large amount of capital investment as a mode of a foreign market entry mode (Lages and Montgomery, 2004; Agndal and Chetty, 2007).

Despite the increased importance of export activities, there are many factors that inhibit many firms from initiating and developing export activities (Leonidou, 2004). The predominance of these barriers, while important, is not a sufficient reason to inhibit the firm's engagement to the internationalization path. Many other factors, identified at the decision maker (Gripsrud, 1990, Roy and Simpson, 1981), organizational (Moon and Lee, 1990) or environmental level, are responsible for making latent barriers to exporting operative and effective. Many researchers in international business has attracted by the negative role that export barrier perceptions can have on the export activity of firms (Kahiya et.al., 2016, Milianzi Mursali, 2012, Arteaga-Ortiz, Jesús, and Rubén Fernández-Ortiz, 2010).

One of the most popular products exported from Greece is the Greek yogurt. In 2007, it accounted for just 1% of US yogurt sales and during the period 2008-2010, Business Insider reported that sales have grown almost 100% each of these years. Now, around half of all yogurt quantities that are sold in the US is Greek. Interest has also spread beyond the US - to Europe, Asia and Australasia - and has inspired a new generation of high-protein 'origin' yogurt products. The demand for Greek yogurt in the US and Europe is high because of their growing passion for healthy eating duo to its high protein and low sugar content and consumers prefer it over other foods, because it is more healthy and nutritious. This increase in demand has boosted the yogurt exports and according to the UBS Investment Research (2011) "Greek yogurt ... have captured market share more quickly than almost any segment in a major food ever...".

Based on the aforementioned, the present paper focuses on the perceptions of export problems faced by Greek yogurt firms. The main objective is to investigate the Greek yogurt manager's perceptions regarding the factors that inhibit their export activities. To this end, the article first reviews and summarizes the relevant literature. It then explains the methodology adopted for carrying out empirical research on the subject. The findings of the study are subsequently analyzed and discussed. Finally, certain conclusions are derived from the research.

2. BARRIERS TO INTERNATIONALIZATION

Barriers to internationalization by exporters and/or non-exporters have attracted the interest of international scholars (e.g. Leonidou, 1995 Morgan, 1997). At an initial stage of internationalization, firms do not have sufficient knowledge on exports and they tend to choose a relatively simple form of market presence in the form of exports. Later on, with experience of export markets, firms tend to take a much more complex form of internationalization like a branch. Nowadays, this approach might not be applicable for large firms as they have access to various kinds of needed information and resources (Gubik & Karajz, 2014,). Exporting does not require large capital investments, and carries less commercial and financial risk than the direct investment forms of internationalization. Yet many firms, especially the ones in developing countries, do not consider exporting as an option (Al-Hyari et al., 2012; Agndal and Chetty, 2007).

Export barriers can be defined as all those that inhibit the firm's ability to initiate or develop business activities in foreign markets (Leonidou 2004). Also, export barriers present problems at three distinct levels. For non-exporting firms, barriers are considered limited and may be the reasons for non export activity (Pinho and Martins 2010). However, export barriers alone prevent a firm from internationalization (Leonidou 2004). Hence, given adequate levels of pre-export planning, in particular, information gathering and resource mobilization, firms can surmount the seemingly limiting undertaking and embark on internationalization.

According to Mavrogiannis et al. (2008), continuing exporters face multiple barriers as they endeavor to gain market share and expand operations. For continuing exporters, export barriers have an inhibitive effect because they limit the strategic options at the firm's disposal. Benito and Welch (1997), refers that persistent export barriers have the propensity to induce "managerial rethink," consequently forcing firms to concern de-internationalization. Hence, export barriers are the reason why firms may discontinue exporting (Crick 2002).

Broadly speaking, export barriers can be classified as internal and external. Internal are barriers associated with organizational resources and company approach to export business, and external, that is barriers stemming from the home and host environment within which the firm operates. Whereas the practical strength of this classification, for analytical purposes internal barriers can be divided further into functional, informational, and marketing, while external barriers can be separated into governmental, task, procedural, and environmental (Figure 1).

Barriers to exporting can be separated among three groups of firms:

1. Non exporters, companies with not exporting activity currently but with future potential,

2. Current exporters, that is, firms currently engaged in export activities, who experience problems with involvement in overseas markets and

3. Ex-exporters, comprising companies that used to export in the past but no longer do so. These firms saw export barriers from both a perceptual and experiential viewpoint.

Several studies have shown that the impact of these two categories of barriers varies widely among these groups, stressing the need for different practice by export promotion programs (Keng and Jiuan 1989, Yaprak 1985). The nature of barrier may be differ markedly from stage to stage but they can be found at any stage of export development process (Naidu and Rao 1993, Vozikis and Mescon 1985). Vozikis and Mescon (1985) found that as small firms become more internationalized and the problems pertaining to the functional areas of marketing, finance, and operations tend to diminish (although management-related export barriers remain high at any stage). Also, it is important to understand problems within each stage of exporting, it is equally important to realize that certain obstacles impede the movement of the firm between export stages. Although constraints play a crucial role in export development, alone they neither will prohibit nor will inhibit the firm's progress in export activity. Other factors are required to make these latent barriers operative, usually associated with the idiosyncratic characteristics of the manager and the environment within which the company operates (Barrett and Wilkinson 1985, Leonidou and Katsikeas 1996). As a result, two firms that are at the same stage of export development may not perceive the same impact from a specific barrier.

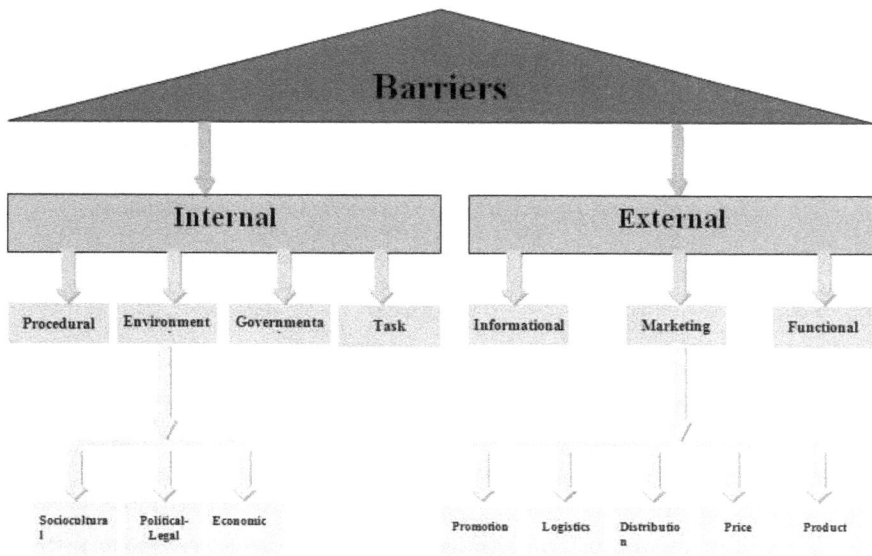

Figure 1. Classification of export barriers according to Leonidou (2004)

Source: adapted from Leonidou (2004, p. 283).

Moreover, the same obstacle may be perceived at different points in time and in relation to different export destination by the same firm. The most important factors in conceptualizing the type, content, and impact of the export barrier are from managers. Firms whose decision managers are rather incompetent and risk-averse are very likely to perceive export obstacles in a more intense and severe manner than firms with capable, risk-taking, and foreign-oriented managers (Dichtl et al., 1990).

Differences in export-barrier impact also can be the outcome of variations in managerial attitudes toward costs, profits, and growth aspects of exporting (Leonidou, Katsikeas, and Piercy 1998). Also, organizational factors may have a discriminating effect on export-barrier perceptions. For example, the firms that have been in the export market for a long time are not sensitive to export barriers, compared to young firms (Leonidou 2000). Moreover, the young firm are more vulnerable it is to barriers associated with resource limitations, operating difficulties, and trade restrictions (Katsikeas and Morgan 1994). Furthermore, appear to perceive export barriers differently by firms belonging to different industries, whether consumer or industrial, (Alexandrides 1971, Kedia and Chhokar 1986).

Finally, environmental factors can affect export-barrier perceptions in two ways:

1. They can be the source of barriers in the home market, such as those connected with the local government, logistics system, and infrastructural facilities, and

2. They shape the obstacles derived from foreign market conditions (such as, economic, political, and sociocultural) within which the firm has to operate.

Table 1. A review of export barriers in various empirical investigations
(Narayanan, Vijay, 2005)

Representative	Research Sample	Barriers typology	Explanation
Leonidou (2004)	Based on an integrative literature review of 32 empirical studies from 1960 – 2000, 39 export barriers were identified (qualitative analysis). The identified barriers were used to get empirical data from 438 firms and conclusions drawn (quantitative analysis)	Internal Barriers 1. Informational 2. Functional 3. Marketing 3.1. Product 3.2. Price 3.3. Distribution 3.4. Logistics 3.5. Promotion External Barriers 1. Procedural 2. Governmental 3. Task 4. Environmental 4.1. Economic 4.2. Political-Legal 4.3. Sociocultural	Study of export barriers in the past has failed to provide a comprehensive overview of export barriers. In an attempt to provide an integrative solution, the author has analyzed 32 empirical studies to provide a unified theory on export barriers. These studies covered diversified regions, industries and firms that intend to export, currently exporting and ex-exporting firms. Problems arising from the internal barriers from the home country are easier to control than problems arising in the host country. Small business managers must act proactively to reduce the effects of these barriers and policy makers should assist exports through awareness and export assisting programs/workshops.
Arteaga–Ortiz & Fernandez-Ortiz (2010)	Based on the literature review of previous studies, the author has classified the different export barriers into four groups primarily because of similarity of the barriers and to homogenize the barriers based on measurement types, scales used etc (qualitative analysis). From this a classification of barriers were arrived. A total of 2,590 questionnaires were sent to Spanish SMEs in 4 macro sectors namely food and agriculture, consumer goods, capital goods and services. A total of 478 valid responses were analyzed with empirical analysis (quantitative analysis).	1. Knowledge Barriers 2. Resource Barriers 3. Procedure Barriers 4.Exogenous Barriers	Knowledge barriers along with lack of information about export assistance programs are a significant export barrier. Resource barriers are barriers that result from the lack of financial resources available within the firm. Resource barriers include insufficient production capacity, lack of credit/finance to support export sales, do market research, lack of local banks, lack of staff for exports, specialists etc. Procedural barriers include bureaucracy, cultural, linguistic and logistical barriers. Exogenous barriers include dy. Statistical evidence confirms the classification of the above mentioned four barrier classification is consistent with the actual practice. uncertainties in the international markets, actions of competitors, governments, exchange rate fluctuations etc. The final questioner used contained 26 variables plus 2 open questions. The conclusions of the study indicated that there was no significantly different barrier other than the ones confirmed in the study. Statistical evidence confirms the

			classification of the above mentioned four barrier classification is consistent with the actual practice.
Arndt, Buch & Mattes (2012)	Theoretical study was used to arrive at a hypothesis (qualitative analysis). The hypothesis was used to collect empirical data from 16,000 German firms (quantitative analysis)	1. Firm Size and productivity 2. Labor market frictions 3. Financial constraints	The study was done based on The firm level data available on firm size, productivity, international activities, access to external capital and labor market frictions. The main findings of this paper are… 1. Firm size and productivity are one of the main determinants of foreign activities of a firm. 2. Labor market frictions affect a firm's decision to invest abroad or export. High hiring and firing cost and other labor market frictions act as barriers to exports. 3. Financial constraints tend not to be major constraints for average German companies.
Leonidou (1995); Morgan (1997)	Literature review based on 35 empirical studies containing 33 studies published in 18 different sources was used to identify export barriers (qualitative). Based on the barrier classification a ranking of frequency was done to in descending order. This data was further analyzed for empirical relationships for different parameters (quantitative analysis).	1, Internal Domestic 2, Internal- Foreign 3, External– Domestic 4. External– Foreign	Barriers from within the firm and relating to the domestic market are called internal barriers. External-domestic: are barriers in the external environment beyond the control of the firm. Internal-foreign is barriers related to the marketing strategy of the firm in the foreign environment. External-foreign is uncontrollable barriers in the foreign environment. The analysis of the empirical relations among previous studies did not provide a uniform pattern in rank and order of export barriers because of various international, national, industry and company specific factors as well as due to different methodologies applied by previous researchers. Availability of information to locate and analyze foreign markets proved to be the major deterrent for Internationalization. To reduce the effect of export barriers concerned managers could use the support of consultancy, advisory and training services.
Kneller et al. (2011)	Empirical Analysis (quantitative analysis) done on data collected from OMB research done in 2005. The samples include firms that took part in UK Trade Investment (UKTI) support program and as control, exporters that did not seek support from UKTI.	1. Trade costs. 1.1. Transport 1.2. Tariff 1.3. Non-Tariff 2. Trade friction. 2.1. Different Languages 2.2. Culture 2.3. Currencies 2.4. Imperfect information 2.5. Incomplete contracts 2.6. Environmental policy.	The initial contact and marketing costs are important barriers to export. The probability that the firms will face these barriers again in the future decreases with increase in export experience. The other important barriers include initial contact with prospective customers and relationship building etc. The probability of facing other barriers like language, information about the foreign market, legal, financial and tax related issues declines with increase in export market experience.

4.   Materials and Methods

During the preliminary stage of the study, 137 manufacturing firms (a complete census) were registered in the Directory of the Hellenic Chamber of Commerce and the Organization of Greek Exporters (2015). Each one firm was contacted by telephone in order to check whether it was still operating and the correctness of its address, to identify the most appropriate individual (key informant) to whom the questionnaire should be addressed and to pre-notify the execution of the study and dispatch the questionnaire, potentially enhancing the response rate (Jobber and O'Reilly, 1998). At a first stage, the questionnaires were mailed to each respondent, filled out by the respondents and mailed back. The initial contact with the target population resulted in 64 fully completed responses (46,7 per cent response rate). During a second stage, two follow-up phone reminders were made to each non-responding firm (73 firms) approximately 3 to 6 weeks after the original mailing, in an attempt to increase the response rate yielding a usable sample of 104 firms (75,91 per cent response rate). Out of these, 20.19% (21 firms) were exporters, thus denoting a relatively export propensity rate among yogurt manufacturing firms in Greece.

5.   Data Analysis

To verify the dimensions and reliability of the constructs, several data purification processes are conducted in this research, including factor analysis(FA), Confirmatory factor analysis, Coefficient alpha analysis (Cronbach's) and Friedman test.

Principal components analysis with varimax rotation was used to reduce the number of export barriers into a few factors. Confirmatory factor analysis was conducted for all constructs to confirm the multi-collinearity among variables, and coefficient alpha accesses the internal consistency of each variable. For each research construct, factor analysis is adopted first to select the items with higher factor loading, and then to compare with the theoretically suggested items. As shown in Table 3, specific criteria as proposed by Hair et al. (2011) for FA, and Arbuckle (1999) in terms of chi-square, goodness of fit index (GFI), adjusted goodness of fit index (AGFI) and root mean square residual (RMR), are fulfilled. For factor analysis, the criteria involved factor loadings greater than 0.5 ~ 0.6, a communality value higher than 0.4, a Kaiser Meyer Olkin measure of sampling adequacy, KMO greater than 0.5 and a Bartlett's test significant of $p < 0.05$, an eigenvalue greater than 1, an explained variance (accumulative) greater than 0.6, while for the reliability test, the Cronbach's alpha (α) greater than 0.7 was followed. As for the confirmatory factor analysis, the criteria included a X^2 – chi-square – small is better $p < 0.05$; $\chi2$ / df < 3, a Goodness of fit index (GFI) > 0.90, an

Adjusted of goodness of fit index (AGFI) > 0.90, an RMR error index less than 0.005 and a RMSEA index of less that0.08 or NFI, CFI, TI indices that are greater than 0.90.

Our export barrier scale had an acceptable Kaiser-Meyer Olkin sampling adequacy (0,712), and the chi-square for Bartlett's test of sphericity was significant. A five-factor solution explaining 68,71% of the variability in the export barrier scale emerged from the analysis. Table 2 shows the detailed results of the FA. Further, we named each of the factors by focusing on the items with the highest loadings and also referring to analogous barrier factors in extant literature (see Da Rocha et al., 2008; Julian and Ahmed, 2005; Leonidou, 2000; Pinho and Martins, 2010). Finally, the non-parametric Friedman test is used to compare the values of correlated groups of variables. The distribution of the Friedman test is χ^2 distribution with degrees of freedom df = k-1, where k is the number of teams or samples. This test classifies the values of variables for every subject separately and calculates the mean rank of classification values for each variable (Freund and Wilson, 2003, Ho, 2006).

6.   Results and discussion

As Table 2 shows the managers of Greek yogurts industry through the application of the Friedman test, whether they export or not, perceive the main five barriers to internationalization as being the large input costs on export markets with a mean rank 16,62, the strict legislation on export markets with a mean rank 15,19, the bureaucracy in government departments with a mean rank 15,13, the lack of capital with a mean rank 14,64 and the late payments by the representatives with a mean rank 14,58 (N= 104 Chi-Square=299,55 df =23 Asymp, Sig = 0,000). The results reaffirm previous literature (e.g. Ward, 1993 Karagozoglu and Lindell 1998, Burpitt and Rondinelli, 2000).

The barriers which are of greatest concern are those relating to large input costs on export markets and lack of capital. For Greek yogurt industry, this is clearly a big issue as younger firms are unlikely to have the same access to capital funds as more established firms. This barrier could be preventing some Greek yogurt industry from internationalizing as much as they might wish. This problem of access to capital and resources for smaller firms is one which has been observed by a number of other researchers (e.g. Fillis, 2001, Rhee, 2002, Coviello and McAuley, 1999, Burpitt and Rondinelli, 2000, Ali and Camp, 1993). Strict legislation on export markets and Bureaucracy in government departments are then perceived to be greater barriers than late payments by the representatives. Other issues identified in earlier studies as barriers to internationalization such as competition in overseas markets (e.g. Leonidou 2004), tariff and non-tariff barriers (Coviello and McAuley, 1999, Karagozoglu and Lindell 1998) did not appear to be such major barriers for Greek yogurt.

Table 2: Friedman test results for evaluating the responsibility regarding the agricultural problems

Export Barriers		Mean Rank
Large input costs on export markets.	**K81**	**16,62**
Strict legislation on export markets.	**K85**	**15,19**
Bureaucracy in government departments	**K100**	**15,13**
lack of capital	**K86**	**14,64**
Late payments by the representatives	**K101**	**14,58**
Limited information about the destination markets.	K84	14,06
Competition in overseas markets	K96	13,91
Poor organization of firm's export department	K98	13,91
Lack of personnel qualified for exporting	K99	13,61
Ineffective national export promotion programs	K102	13,61
Difficulties with intermediaries	K94	13,01
Foreign tariff barriers	K82	12,90
Exchange rate instability.	K83	12,89
High customer demands	K103	12,85
High transportation costs	K104	12,74
Quality/Product Features/Lifetime of product	K93	12,39
Distrust generally on the Greek economy	K95	11,42
Unfriendly Domestic Legislation.	K87	11,23
Difficulty participating in international distribution networks	K90	10,85
Lack of competitive prices	K97	9,87
Politically unstable of export markets	K91	9,46
Language problems	K88	9,33
Prices of competing products	K89	8,45
Lack of skilled labor.	K92	7,36

N = 104, Chi-Square = 299,55, df = 23, Asymp. Sig = 0,000

A factor analysis (FA) was undertaken in order to assess how the barriers to internationalization are related to each other. All 24 barriers were fed into a principal components analysis to assess the psychometric properties of the instrument assessing barriers to export identified as export market attractiveness, foreign practices being incompatible with domestic business, export venture management characteristics, distribution access, adapting to foreign market needs and government policy. Our primary concern was interpretability of the factors. All items loaded appropriately and no cross loadings above 0.2 were identified with only factor loadings of above 0.5 being accepted (Table 3). Each scale was reviewed using factor analysis to establish that they were unidimensional. The final reliabilities for all scales were greater than 0.50 in all cases with a few over 0.80. The five factors explained 68,71 percent of respondent variation on issues about the barriers to export confronting export market ventures (Table 3).

The first factor comprised competition in overseas markets (K96), foreign tariff barriers (K82), exchange rate instability (K83), politically unstable of export markets (K91) and difficulties with intermediaries (K94). Exchange rate instability and foreign trade barriers were the variables mostly contributed to this factor that mostly refers to barriers from the external environment of the firm. Furthermore, this factor explained 30,94% of the variance, with an eigenvalue of 4.951 and a Cronbach's α of 0.814 and can be defined as *"Foreign restrictions and standards (EP1)".*

The second factor comprised the bureaucracy in government departments (K100), language problems (K88), the poor organization of firm's export department (K98) and the lack of personnel qualified for exporting (K99). The poor organization of export departments and the bureaucracy in government departments are the variables that loaded more significantly to his particular factor, which mainly involves Procedural Barriers. This factor explained 11.90% of the variance, with an eigenvalue of 1.904 and a Cronbach's α of 0.811 and can be defined as *"Deficiency of export department (EP2)".*

The third factor consisted of the ineffective national export promotion programs (K102), the large input costs on export markets (K81) and the lack of capital (K86). The particular factor used to measure Governmental Barriers, with the lack of capital making the highest loading to this factor. Furthermore, the factor explained 11.54% of the variance, with an eigenvalue of 1.847 and a Cronbach's α of 0.7 and may be defined as *'Incomplete Promotion Product (EP4)".*

The last factor comprised the High transportation costs (K104), the difficulty participating in international distribution networks (K90) and the quality of product (Product Features/Lifetime of product) (K93), which loaded most significantly. This factor mainly referred to Trade Barriers and explained 7.59% of the variance, with an eigenvalue of 1.214 and a Cronbach's α of 0.578 and can be defined as *"Product transfer restrictions (EP4)".*

Table 3: Factor Analysis Results - Confirmatory Factor Analyses: Standardized Loading (ML estimations), Measure Reliabilities

Code	Name of construct-Item tapping each construct		Factor loading	Eigenvalue	Variance (%)	Goodness-of-fit	Standardized path coefficients*
EP1	Competition in overseas markets	K96	0,736	4,951	30,94	X2: 90,775 , df: 72 , p: 0,067 , CFI: 0,967 , RMSEA: 0,5, Reliability: 0,814	1
	Foreign tariff barriers	K82	0,751				0,494
	Exchange rate instability	K83	0,785				0,624
	Politically unstable of export markets	K91	0,705				0,597
	Difficulties within intermediaries	K94	0,621				0,826
EP2	Bureaucracy in government departments	K100	0,759	1,904	11,90	X2: 90,775 , df: 72 , p: 0,067 , CFI: 0,967 , RMSEA: 0,5 , Reliability: 0,811	1
	Language problems	K88	0,744				0,449
	Poor organization of firm's export department	K98	0,787				0,747
	Lack of personnel qualified for exporting	K99	0,744				0,945
EP3	Ineffective national export promotion programs	K102	0,618	1,847	11,54	X2: 90,775 , df: 72 , p: 0,067 , CFI: 0,967 , RMSEA: 0,5 , Reliability: 0,700	1
	Large input costs on export markets.	K81	0,729				0,699
	Lack of capital	K86	0,832				0,604
EP4	High transportation costs	K104	0,631	1,214	7,56	X2: 90,775 , df: 72 , p: 0,067 , CFI: 0,967 , RMSEA: 0,5 , Reliability: 0,578	1
	Difficulty participating in international distribution networks	K90	0,758				0,329
		K93	0,790				0,438
	Quality/Product Features/Lifetime of product						
EP5	Unfriendly Domestic Legislation	K87	0,842	1,079	6,75		

The fifth factor included only one item, the unfriendly domestic legislation and was referred to measure Marketing Barriers. The particular factor explained 6.75% of the total variance, with an eigenvalue of 1.079 and may be defined as *"Domestic Legislation (EP5)".*

7. Conclusion

The present study investigated the barriers that Greek yogurt firms confront when engaged in export activities. Primary data were gathered based on a survey of 104 Greek yogurt manufacturing firms and the results revealed several useful insights. Specifically, the large input costs on export markets, the strict legislation on export markets, the bureaucracy in government departments, the lack of capital and the late payments by distributors were the major barriers to export, as perceived by managers. The study's results may consist a platform for state policy makers to implement related policy measures and export promotion programs to enhance the internationalization of yogurt firms. The efficiency of these programs is intimately related to both (a) the identification of target firms for such programs – normally exporting companies and non-exporting which are interested in exporting (Yang, 1988) – and with an appropriate segmentation of them, and (b) the awareness of firms' different needs with respect to internationalization, all of which involve different forms of support programs. This study contributes to both of these aspects. Conclusively, the study has, at this stage, focused on perceptions of barriers. Possible avenues for future research may include the influence of both attitudes towards international expansion and entrepreneurial orientation on the perceptions of the barriers to internationalization.

References

Agndal, H. and Chetty, S. (2007), "The impact of relationships on changes in internationalisation strategies of SMEs", European Journal of Marketing, Vol. 41 Nos 11/12, pp. 1449-74.

Alexandrides, C.G. (1971), "How the major obstacles to exporting can be overcome", Atlantic Economic Review, May, pp. 12-15

Al-Hyari, K., Al-Weshah, G., & Alnsour, M. (2012). Barriers to internationalisation in SMEs: evidence from Jordan. Marketing Intelligence & Planning, 30(2), 188-211.

Ali, A.J. and Camp, R.C. (1993). The relevance of firm size and international business experience to market entry strategies. Journal of Global Marketing. 6(4), 91-108.

Andersson, S. and Flore´n, H. (2008), "Exploring managerial behavior in small international firms", Journal of Small Business and Enterprise Development, Vol. 15 No. 1, pp. 31-50.

Arteaga-Ortiz, Jesús, and Rubén Fernández-Ortiz. "Why don't we use the same export barrier measurement scale? An empirical analysis in small and medium-sized enterprises." Journal of Small Business Management 48.3 (2010): 395-420.

Barrett, Nigel I., and Ian F. Wilkinson (1985). "Export Stimulation: A Segmentation Study of the Exporting Problems of Australian Manufacturing Firms," European Journal of Marketing 19(2), 53–72.

Benito GRG, Welch LS (1997) De-internationalization. ManagInt Rev 37(2):7–25

Burpitt, W.J. and Rondinelli, D.A. (2000). Small firms' motivations for exporting: To earn and learn? Journal of Small Business Management, October, 1-14.

Coviello, N.E. and McAuley, A. (1999). Internationalization and the smaller firm: A review of contemporary empirical research. Management International Review, 39(3), 223-256.

Crick D (2002) The decision to discontinue exporting: SMEs in two U.K. trade sectors. J Small Bus Manag 40(1):66–77

Da Rocha, A., Freitas, Y., & Da Silva, J. (2008). Do perceived barriers change over time? A longitudinal study of Brazilian exporters of manufactured goods. Latin American Business Review, 9(1), 102–108.

Dichtl, Erwin, Hans-Georg Köglmayr, and Stefan Müller (1990). "International Orientation as a Precondition for Export Success," Journal of International Business Studies 21(1), 23–40.

Fillis, I. (2001). Small firm internationalisation: An investigative survey and future directions. Management Decision. 39(9), 767-783

Freund, R., and Wilson, W., 2003, Statistical methods (New York: Elsevier).

Gripsrud, G. (1990), "The determinants of export decisions and attitudes to a distant market: Norwegian fishery exports to Japan", Journal of International Business Studies, Vol. 21 No. 3, pp. 469-85.

Gubik, Andrea S., and SándorKarajz. "The Choice of Foreign Market Entry Modes: The Role of Resources and Industrial Driving Forces1." Entrepreneurial Business and Economics Review 2.1 (2014): 49.

Hair, J.F., Ringle, C.M. and Sarstedt, M. (2011) 'PLS-SEM: indeed a silver bullet', The Journal of Marketing Theory and Practice, Vol. 19, No. 2, pp.139–152.

Ho, R., 2006, Handbook of Univariate and Multivariate Data Analysis and Interpretation with SPSS (USA: Chapman & Hall).

Jobber D, O'Reilly D. Industrial mail surveys: a methodological update. Ind Mark Manage 1998;2:95–107

Julian, C. C., & Ahmed, Z. U. (2005). The impact of barriers to export on export marketing performance. Journal of Global Marketing, 19(1), 71–94.

Kahiya, Eldrede T., and David L. Dean. "Export Stages and Export Barriers: Revisiting Traditional Export Development." Thunderbird International Business Review 58.1 (2016): 75-89.

Karagozoglu, N. and Lindell, M. (1998). Internationalization of small and medium-sized technology-based firms: An exploratory study. Journal of Small Business Management. January, 44-59.

Kedia, B.L. and Chhokar, J. (1986), "Factors inhibiting export performance of firms: an empirical investigation", Management International Review, Vol. 26 No. 4, pp. 33-43

Keng, K.A. and Jiuan, T.S. (1989), "Differences between small and medium sized exporting and non-exporting firms: nature and nurture", International Marketing Review, Vol. 6 No. 4, pp. 27-40.

Koksal, M.H. (2006), "Export training: a preliminary investigation of Turkish companies", European Business Review, Vol. 18 No. 5, pp. 382-94. Koksal, M.H. (2008), "How export marketing research affects company export performance: evidence from Turkish companies", Marketing Intelligence & Planning, Vol. 26 No. 4, pp. 416-30.

Lages, L.F. and Montgomery, A.D.B. (2004), "Export performance as an antecedent of export commitment and marketing strategy adaptation: evidence from small and medium-sized exporters", European Journal of Marketing, Vol. 38 Nos 9/10, pp. 1186-214.

Leonidou, L. C. (2000). Barriers to export management: An organizational and internationalization analysis. Journal of International Management, 6(2), 121–148. Leonidou, L. C. (2004). An analysis of the barriers hindering small export development. Journal of Small Business Management, 42(3), 279–303.

Leonidou, Leonidas C. "An analysis of the barriers hindering small business export development." Journal of small business management 42.3 (2004): 279-302.

Mavrogiannis M, Bourlakis MA, Dawson PJ, Ness MR (2008) Assessing export performance in the Greek food and beverage industry: an integrated structural equation approach. Br Food J 110(7):638–654

Milanzi, Mursali A. "Export barrier perceptions in Tanzania: The influence of social networks." Journal of African Business 13.1 (2012): 29-39.

Moon, J. and Lee, H. (1990), "On the internal correlates of export stage development: an empirical investigation in the Korean electronics industry", International Marketing Review, Vol. 7 No. 5, pp. 16-26

Morgan RE, Katsikeas CS (1998) Exporting problems of industrial manufacturers. Ind Mark Manag 27:161–176

Naidu, G. M., and T. R. Rao (1993). "Public Sector Promotion of Exports: A Needs-Based Approach," Journal of Business Research 27(31), 85–101

Narayanan, Vijay. "Export Barriers for Small and Medium-sized Enterprises: A Literature Review based on Leonidou's Model." Entrepreneurial Business and Economics Review 3.2 (2015): 105.

Papalexiou, Christos. "Barriers to the export of Greek wine." 113th EAAE Seminar: A Resilient European Food Industry and Food Chain in a Challenging World, Chania, Crete, G Zimmermann, C. and Kattuman, P.A. (2007), "On 'considering' internationalization: how do perceived resource-based constraints matter?", Working Paper Series 07/2007, Cambridge Judge Business School, Cambridge.reece, September. 2009.

Pinho, J. C., & Martins, L. (2010). Exporting barriers: Insights from Portuguese small-and-medium sized exporters and non-exporters. Journal of International Entrepreneurship, 8, 254–272.

Rhee, J.H. (2002). An exploratory examination of propensity and performance in new venture internationalization. New England Journal of Entrepreneurship. 51-66.

Roy, D.A. and Simpson, C.L. (1981), "Attitudes toward exporting in the smaller manufacturing firm", Journal of Small Business Management, Vol. 19 No. 2, pp. 16-22.

United States International Trade Commission (2010), Small and Medium-Sized Enterprises: Overview of Participation in US Exports, USITC Publication 4125, United States International Trade Commission, Washington, DC

Vozikis, George S., and Timothy S. Mescon (1985). "Small Exporters and Stages of Development: An Empirical Study," American Journal of Small Business (Summer), 49–64

Ward, E.A. (1993). Motivation of expansion plans of entrepreneurs and small business managers. Journal of Small Business Management. January, 32-38.

Yaprak, A. (1985), "An empirical study of the differences between small exporting and nonexporting US firms", International Marketing Review, Vol. 2 No. 2, Summer, pp. 72-83.

Chapter 7

EXPLORING THE DIFFERENCES IN THE DEVELOPMENT OF RURAL AREAS IN BOSNIA AND HERZEGOVINA

Nataša Tandir[1] and Zafer Konakli[2]

[1]International Burch University, Francuske Revolucije bb, 71000 Sarajevo, Bosnia and Herzegovina, natasa.tandir@ibu.edu.ba

[2]International Burch University, Francuske Revolucije bb, 71000 Sarajevo, Bosnia and Herzegovina, zafer.konakli@ibu.edu.ba

ABSTRACT

There is a strong need for efficient measurements and policies in development of rural areas mainly because they contribute to regions prosperity and they have a potential to generate growth as dynamic urban areas.

In Bosnia and Herzegovina some rural municipalities with similar population density are very different regarding key demographic and economic indicators like migration, unemployment and average wages. Likewise, data about unemployment do not show any kind of pattern that could explain those differences. So far, studies in the country have not identified low and high performing rural areas (municipalities) and evaluated the factors, (so called capitals, or assets) for those disparities among them.

According to the existing studies in Europe the answer for differential economic performance is firstly in the potential of local community to recognise, strengthen and utilise less mobile assets in the form of economic, social, cultural and natural capital. Secondly, researchers point to the synergy between those assets and external networking and using information and communications technology in reaching new markets and resources.

Understanding the reasons for differential economic performance and more or less competitiveness in rural areas of Bosnia and Herzegovina could thus be a key element in devising practical strategies and programmes for sustainable rural development. This could also contribute to the programming of IPARD for Bosnia and Herzegovina in the future.

The aim of the study is by comparing the most and least developed rural municipalities to investigate the reasons for the differences in economic performance, in particular, to investigate the role of capitals or tangible and less tangible factors influencing development outcomes. Additional aim is to draw lessons from examples of successful communities and to propose measures for policy makers in order to improve socio-economic status of less successful communities. In order to achive that, the authors have chosen high and low performing municipalities according to the criteria of population density, rurality and proximity to large city. In order to have more clear picture, community profiling is conducted and data was collected by surveying community stakeholders.

The analysis showed that in high performing municipality all capitals are accessible and properly utilised with space for improvement while low performing municipality has many problems and higher need for change and new strategy of development.

KEYWORDS

Rural development, community capitals, municipality.

JEL CLASSIFICATION CODES

R11, D63

1. INTRODUCTION

For many years, rural was associated with population decline, degradation of the countryside, population aging, gender inequality, increased unemployment and poverty. However, literature gives some evidence that the mentioned image of rural Europe needs re-shaping (OECD, 1996; Bollman and Bryden, 1997; European Commission (EC), 1997; Terluin and Post, 2000).

According to Dower (2013), when writing about European Union, there is a strong need for efficient measurements and policies in development of rural areas mainly for two reasons. First is that rural areas "contribute to Europe's prosperity". For decades, rural areas have provided most of the natural resources upon which an increasingly urbanised Europe depends (Ministry of Regional Development, 2011; Dower, 2013, Wakeford, 2013). They have provided also the necessary skills for exploitation, processing and transportation of these resources. Since there is a growing need for natural resources, and their usage in modern and sustainable way, the role of rural areas is very important. Other important fact is gross social and economic disparities between rural regions compared to urban and other rural areas.

However, there are studies that show different results. According to OECD (1996, 2006, 2012) there are peripheral areas that perform good or even better than urban areas which leads to the concept of "differential performance" between rural areas which exist in relatively similar conditions related to geography, location, available natural resources, policies, etc. It is obvious that traditional theories (core-periphery or neo-classical) or "new economic geography" related to rural-urban development processes, cannot explain those performance differences of rural areas with similar characteristics (Krugman, 1993, 1999; Kilkenny, 1993, 1998, 1999).

Authors Bryden and Munro (2000) emphasize that the answer is firstly in the potential of local community to recognize, strengthen and utilize less mobile assets in the form of economic, social, cultural and natural capital. Secondly, researchers point to the synergy between those assets and external networking and using information and communications technology in reaching new markets and resources.

The identification of barriers and opportunities is important for planning and creating adequate policies that will address these problems and challenges. Examining the available capitals in the two types of communities, successful and less successful, would provide information about possibilities on one side and limitations on the other. Concentrating on what rural areas have rather on what they need is acknowledged approach in assessing potentials for local/regional development.

Bosnia and Herzegovina is one of the most rural countries in Europe. More than 60 percent of its population lives in rural areas. There are few studies about the socio-economic indicators of regions in BiH.[9] Some of the results indicate that the rural municipalities with similar population density are very different regarding key demographic and economic indicators like migration, unemployment and average wages. Data about unemployment do not show any kind of pattern that could explain those differences. According to the estimation of UN (2010), there are significant regional disparities in BH. Out of 142 municipalities, 89 are undeveloped or extremely undeveloped. The same study identified five best ranked regions: Sarajevo, Hercegovacko-neretvanski canton, East Sarajevo, Banja Luka and Zenica-Doboj canton. Five least ranked regions are Kanton 10, Unasana canton, Bosnia-Podrinje canton, Posavski canton and Bijeljina.

This raises the question why some municipalities have such low indicators and how their problems can be solved. Especially, this can be answered by looking at the communities that are creating jobs, raising incomes, attracting migrants...

---

[9] BiH Regional Disparity Assessment 2010; UNDP, 2013, Socio-ekonomski pokazatelji po opcinama u FBiH, 2009, 2010, 2011, 2012, 2013, 2014

What is the secret of their success and how can it be replicated to the rest of the country?

According to the above mentioned, case study analysis of some of the best and worst ranked municipalities in the country, according to the development index, would provide useful information for future rural development of Bosnia and Herzegovina.

The main contribution of this research is that it is making the distinction between indicators that "measure performance" and the ones that help "explain" relatively good or bad performance of rural areas. This research is focusing on the later ones which can help local, regional and national policy creators to account for those differences. Understanding the reasons for differential economic performance and more or less competitiveness in rural areas could thus be a key element in devising practical strategies and programmes for sustainable rural development.

The **aim of the study** is by comparing the most and least developed rural municipalities to investigate the reasons for the differences in economic performance, in particular, to investigate the role of capitals or tangible and less tangible factors influencing development outcomes.

The main research question could be stated as: Why do rural areas in apparently similar economic, social and environmental conditions have markedly different performance over relatively longer time periods?

2.   Literature Review

The communities should build on the things that they have rather than concentrate on what they lack. Every community has a set of unique attributes that could form the basis of community and economic security (Braithwaite, 2009).

In the past, activities to define the opportunities for and constraints on development tended to concentrate on deficiencies in physical infrastructure and buildings, including mainly "hard" features of capital creation. Gradually, it came to be recognised that the "soft" aspects of development are equally important and that issues like skills and capacities of the local workforce, its entrepreneurial culture, the effectiveness of business networks and innovativeness, the quality of local institutions and regional governance are crucial components of local territorial assets. This shift in perspective is also visible in the thematic focus of international research, including that of the OECD. The New Rural Paradigm (OECD, 2006) provides a framework that includes substantial perspectives for rural policy.

A conceptual model was created for this study which assumes that the different economic performance of rural areas is the result, in part at least, of five locally available capitals: (1) economic capital; (2) human capital; (3) social capital (4) cultural capital; and (5) environmental capital (natural and built)

2.1. Natural capital

Natural capital represents the basis of the community's assets. Although, it can be easily noticed, it is not always easy to measure natural capital or determine its impact in relation to community development (Russo, 2003; Fey, Bregendahl, and Flora, 2006).

Prugh et al. (1999) stated that the limiting factor of development wouldn't be manufactured capital but natural capital. Few years before Goodland and Daly (1996) stated the same fact. The natural capital shouldn't be considered a free good, "but should be calculated as a limiting factor in development".

It is important to have in mind that the term natural capital includes wider consideration than simply natural resources. An area to be endowed with natural resources is not sufficient asset that can affect rural development. This was elaborated in the study by Ida Terluin (2003) which included 18 case studies in leading and lagging rural regions in the EU. It appeared that there is no significant relationship between being a leading region and endowed with natural resources. However, related to rural amenities (which included some natural assets of high nature value and protected areas like regional or national parks) the relationship seemed to exist. However, the existence of amenities was not the determining factor, but the degree of effective valorisation of those assets. The research showed that some of the rural regions classified as leading have properly exploited their potentials and have developed effective integrated strategies for promoting and marketing those assets.

Development, which conserves and protects natural capital, requires rural communities to develop planning decisions that focus on renewable and non-renewable resources, waste capacity, and the maintenance of biodiversity.

2.2. Built capital

Along with other forms of capital, many studies have highlighted built capital as one of the major contributors to economic development. Built capital, often referred as infrastructure or physical capital, can be defined as physical infrastructure used to support community activities (Crowe, 2006).

Whitener and Parker (2007) imply that the building and expansion of infrastructure holds the most promise for the well-being of rural communities.

Crowe (2009) states that communities with well-managed, high quality built capital have better chance for economic development. Flora et al. (2004) agrees that when infrastructure is available, individuals and businesses are more likely to be productive. Copus et al. (2006) emphasize that infrastructure and access to basic services is of great importance especially in areas with negative population movements or structural economic change.

Investment in rural infrastructure not only benefits the rural community and its residents, it also facilitates the creation of new business and survival and growth of existing ones. Built capital is easy to measure since it is physically present and appraised.

According to the literature, there are four major aspects of built capital that need to be considered when evaluating differences in economic performance of rural areas: transport infrastructure, business-oriented infrastructure, consumer-oriented infrastructure (or basic services), and tourism-related infrastructure.

2.3. Social Capital

Putnam's (1995) definition of social capital is one of the most quoted in modern literature. He defines social capital as: "features of social organisation, such as networks, norms and social trust that facilitate coordination and cooperation for mutual benefit."

Frequently used method in analyzing and discussing social capital is its division into components: bonding, bridging and occasionally linking (Putnam, 2000).

Social capital research encompasses a wide spectrum of topics within the very broad field of social and economic inequality (Brough, 2007). Social capital is measured as an individual, group or organisation and a collective (community-level) attribute (Acquaah et al., 2014).

The measures of social capital and the economic growth are varying across the studies (Westlund and Adam, 2009).

Acquaah et al. (2014) analyzed 314 articles published in the period 1990-2013 in academic and practitioner journals as well as other sources, such as reports from the World Bank. They made a systematic review of definitions, measurements, and values that social capital provides to individuals, businesses and communities. According to their analysis research suggests that the measurement of social capital is multidimensional, and the various components could be summarised into four groups: social networks, trust and reciprocity, norms and civic engagement.

Westlund and Adam (2009) in their evaluation of 65 studies related to social capital come to the conclusion that it is still hard to determine what is the exact level and way of social capital impact on economic development. In their conclusion, they state that social capital induces co-operation, serves as intermediary in interaction with other capitals and creates the basis for dynamic and creative environment.

2.4. Human Capital

Human capital represents the skills and abilities of people in the community. Contemporary understanding of human capital can be attributed to Becker (1964) who refer to it as "the value added to a laborer when the laborer acquires knowledge, skills and other assets useful to the employer or firm in the production and exchange processes". More recent definitions of human capital indicate that it is related to the stock of skills, qualifications and knowledge that individuals possess.

Many researchers state that human capital represents one of the key assets that influences rural economic development (Agarwal et al., 2009; Bryden, 2003; Porter 1990; Reimer 2005, Tweten, 2008).

During the years, different authors have emphasised a number of factors that comprise human capital and that are influencing economic performance of regions and among them rural areas. Identified are: education and skills, leadership, entrepreneurship, demography, migration, access to services, housing, quality of life, rural-urban interactions (Terluin, 2003). Each of these identified factors has number of aspects and all of them can be considered firstly as an input into the production process. The relationship between them is different as well as the influence on the performance level of an area (Agarwal et al., 2009)

2.5. Cultural Capital

Cultural capital has a range of definitions, many of which contrast each other. Matarasso (1999) states that it represents one aspect of human capital that can be obtained through education, training and cultural activities. Agarwal et al. (2009) cites Gould who "considers it to be a form of social capital that is generated when the sharing of culture through celebrations, rites and intercultural dialogue for example, enhances relationships, partnerships and networks within a community". Geertz (1993) describes cultural capital as identity of people and communities they live in, which includes history, traditions, customs, language, art, music and stories associated with the place. Many authors agree that cultural capital consists of community symbols, traditions, language patterns, festivals, celebrations, and other events (Flora et al., 2004; Fritz, Boren, Trudeau, & Wheeler, 2007).

In DORA project (Bryden and Hart, 2001) 'culture' includes local traditions, identity, values and beliefs, attitudes, religion, history and leadership as well as political beliefs and allegiances. All these aspects are expected to indirectly influence economic performance of rural areas.

According to Dower (2013) typical culture of an area can: develop strong sense of identity and pride and create important component for the community members to take initiative in local development; enrich the life of residents; strengthen the local economy by attracting in-migrants and tourists.

The importance of cultural capital in economic development of rural areas is increasing. Cultural activities are usually related to tourism, heritage and historical and local identity. Possibilities for creating economic benefits range from importance of cultural activities and creative industries in attracting innovators, talents, companies and tourists to the role of creativity as resource of local and regional production. However, Copus et al. (2006) indicated that we are lacking information on the significance of cultural activities in rural areas to development, more specific, employment. The existing statistical tools, for example in EU, are not appropriate to capture this sector properly and to enable comparability.

2.6. Economic capital

Economic capital refers to "capital resources that are invested and mobilised in pursuit of profit" (Lin 2001, p.3); It includes investment in production that needs recruiting and organising labour, facilities, equipment and so on, entrepreneurship and innovation. Along with that, it has a social notion. Thus, economic linkages, which include supply chains and local food networks, formal and informal networks are also important for the rural development.

In order to determine the important aspects of economic capital in rural areas it is important to acknowledge two main drivers related to the production and consumption. Firstly, the changes which include moving production away from agriculture towards services or small scale manufacturing activities or from conventional towards modern, technologically advanced agriculture. Second driver are the changes occurring in consumption as a result of income rise, which leads to more spending on non-conventional agricultural and food products, tourism, recreational and cultural activities and concern about the quality of life. These drivers combined with adaptation and implementations of ICT, along with the increased investment in human capital create entrepreneurial opportunities and induce entrepreneurship in rural areas (Copus et al, 2011).

In many countries of EU, rural self-employment becomes vital for economic development of many less-favoured or lagging rural areas (Skuras & Stathopoulou 2000, Copus et al, 2011). Social and economic composition of rural areas can be a driver or a barrier for self-employment. However, sufficient support and focus are necessary for creating new job opportunities. It is important to note that the goals of rural entrepreneurs may be little bit different of those in urban areas. The first goal could be sense of independence, providing jobs for family members, doing something for the community and not mainly profit maximization.

Some of the drivers mentioned in EDORA project (2011) are: the need to diversify supply; progress in food manufacturing, ICTs, packaging and logistics, growing cooperation with R&D institutions; and business cluster creation. Clusters of businesses greatly contribute to the regional economy. It can be defined ad geographically close group of companies and relevant institutions from the same field including producers, service providers, suppliers, research institutions, universities which are complementarily interconnected. Rosenfeld calls rural clusters and networks the "Yin and Yang of Rural Development" (cited in Copus et al, 2011).

3.   METHODOLOGY

The first step was to identify the most and least developed rural areas in FBH using development index, percentage of people living in rural municipalities, population density and proximity to the large urban centre.

In Federation of Bosnia and Hercegovina there are 79 municipalities. Each year Federal Development Planning Institution is evaluating socioeconomic development of each municipality using statistical data and averages which are provided by municipalities and performed by groups of experts so high accuracy and reliability would be achieved. The indicators that are being used are:

- Estimated Gross Domestic Product per capita for each municipality;
- Employment rate
- Unemployment rate
- Number of students of primary and secondary education per 1000 inhabitants
- Absent population compared to the 1991 Census data

Employment rate is established according to the municipality's data about number of employed compared to the estimated number of inhabitants.

Unemployment rate is established according to the municipality's data about the number of unemployed people compared to the active population.

Absent population is established according to the present population compared to the 1991 Census data in municipalities which are a part of Federation of Bosnia and Herzegovina according to the Dayton Agreement.

Selection of case studies (municipalities) eligible for research was conducted in four steps, according to the following criteria:

Municipality development index. For each municipality, five indexes were assigned compared to the average data of the Federation. Summing individual indexes led to the formation of total index of development for each municipality. Appendix 1 presents best and worst ranked municipalities in year 2014 in Federation of Bosnia and Herzegovina.

Level of rurality. The data for determining rurality were taken from the official web site with preliminary statistical data on 2013 Census (see appendix). The column presents the percentage of people living in urban areas.

Population density. The OECD definition of rural areas distinguishes 2 hierarchical levels of territorial unit, local and regional. At local community level (administrative or statistical units- equivalent to NUTS5), the OECD identifies rural areas as communities with a population density below 150 inhabitants per square kilometre. At regional level (aggregated sub-national regions- equivalent to NUTS3), the OECD distinguishes larger functional or administrative units by their degree of rurality, depending on which share of the region's population lives in rural communities. This typology only reflects the degree of rurality of the whole region (OECD, 1996).

To facilitate the analysis, regions are clustered into three types:

1. Predominantly Rural Regions: over 50% of the population living in rural communities;

2. Significantly Rural Regions: 15 to 50% of the population living in rural communities;

3. Predominantly Urban Regions: less than 15% of the population living in rural communities.

According to above mentioned the one column in appendix was created so the intermediate and predominantly urban regions would be excluded from this research.

Proximity to the large city. One more factor according to which case studies are chosen is proximity to the large city. Large cities in BH are considered the ones that have approximately 100,000 inhabitants or even more. In that group are Sarajevo, Banja Luka, Tuzla, Zenica, Mostar and Bijeljina.

Remote rural regions face a different set of problems than rural regions close to a city, where a wider range of services and opportunities can be found (Dijkstra and Ruiz, 2010). According to that, predominantly rural regions close to the city (less than 40 minutes ride) are excluded from the study.

To study socio-economic disparities in chosen rural municipalities, community profiling was conducted by using semi-structured interviews with rural development experts, consulting the news articles in the local newspapers, researching the official statistical data, scanning the web sites of chosen communities, local businesses, and observations made at community events and activities.

4. RESULTS

According to the data presented in appendix two predominantly rural municipalities with the highest and lowest development index, which are satisfying abovementioned criteria are Zepce (high development index) and Bosansko Grahovo (lowest development index). Both case studies are marked at the following figure.

Figure 1. Map of BH with marked case studies

4.1 MUNICIPALITY ZEPCE

Zepce is located in central part of BH and Zenica-Doboj Canton with the area of 282 km². It has 46 settlements with the total population of 31.067. Compared to

Bosansko Grahovo it is smaller in territory but much larger in number of inhabitants (table 1).

Table 1 Main indicators for selected case studies

Indicators	Municipality Zepce Zenica Doboj Canton	Municipality Bosansko Grahovo Canton 10 Livno
Area	282 km2	780 km2
Number of settlements	41	35
Natural resources	63% under forests, 27 km of river Bosna, mineral waters	36,42% under forests, peat, gravel, sand; some under mines
Population	31.067 (4.800 in urban area)	1.996
Working age population 15-64 years of age (%)	70	53,1
Population density	110 per km2	2,6 per km2
Natural population increase	38	-28
Unemployment rate	52,2%	46,9
Women in unemployment rate	46,5%	N/A
Employment rate	14,7%	17,4%
Average salary (KM)	559	986
GDP per capita (KM)	2.210	8.597
Number of people per doctor	1.553	Health care staff is transferred to neighboring municipality Drvar
Number of firms per 1000 inhabitants	39,1	114,7
Regional roads (km)	31	111
Local asphalted roads (km)	113,35	204
Local unpaved roads (km)	88,75	130
Railways (km)	19 (low utilization)	2,5
Price of water/m3 not including VAT (in KM)	0,85 for households 2,40 for business	Average price 2,00
Waste management	5.500 t of waste per year produced (only 20% effectively removed on legal dumping site)	500 t of waste per year, not removed with regular channels
Illegal waste dumping sites	11 macro > 100 micro	2 macro
Suppliers of electricity	2	1
Industrial zones	6	No
Business incubator	1+1 (agro incubator)	No
Kindergarten	1	No
Primary schools	5	1
Secondary schools	3	No
Restaurants	9 (3 with accommodation)	No accommodation capacity
Banks	6 + 2 microcredit organizations	No
Public media	2 local radio stations, 6 web portals with local info	1 official municipality web portal
Clubs	10 cultural societies and 17 sport clubs/societies	3 cultural societies, 1 sport club

Sources: United Nations Trust Fund for Human Security 2015, Nacrt strategije razvoja opstine Bosansko Grahovo (Strategy of Development of Municipality Bosansko Grahovo 2016-2020 - Draft Version); Strategija razvoja opcine Zepce 2011-2018, Razvojna Agencija Zepce, 2011; Socio-ekonomski pokazatelji po opcinama u Federacija Bosne i Herzegovine u 2014. godini, Federal Development Planning Institution, 2015

Related to natural resources municipality has significant number of springs with mineral and drinking water. The territory under forest is governed by three public companies from the Canton, neighbouring municipality Zavidovici and Zepce municipality.

Human capital represents a potential for the municipality. However, the trends and forecasts accordingly imply that certain demographic measures need to be implemented in order to keep positive numbers related to age structure and natural population increase rate.

High unemployment rate (52,2%, table 1) can be explained by deficit in some occupations (bricklayers, carpenters, bar benders, operators of construction machinery, gas welders, ferrymen, language and mathematics professors, doctors) and suficit in some others, low level of qualifications and low number of opportunities for prequalification. Likewise, around 41 per cent of unemployed are older than 40 and this group is characterized as long-term unemployed with "threatened existence and injured pride", since there is no demand for their occupations or skills anymore.

When it comes to education, relevant institutions (kindergarten, primary and secondary schools) exist, however there is a need for major reconstruction and new facilities like sport halls. In order to improve the quality of education human capital engaged in schools needs improvement. It is very important to plan the education program according to the problems and needs of the region. The nearest universities are located in Doboj and Zenica.

Road infrastructure needs improvements because it is overloaded. On the other hand, railway potential for the local and Canton transport is not utilized. Water supply is well managed in the urban part of the municipality and the price of this service (table 1) is among the lowest in Canton. However, the water network is very old (more than 70 years) and is not covering the rural part of the municipality (33 settlements). Rural settlements have their own private solutions for the water supply. There is no adequate organized control of the consumption of water and no statistical data related to different categories of consumers. The sewerage network is characterized by low coverage and lack of statistical data. The waste removal is poorly managed especially in rural areas, with low coverage and lack of adequate infrastructure. There are two phone operators and three mobile operators with good infrastructure and service. However, the residents consider the prices too high.

The local government has no direct influence on the economy, however it can improve and promote the development of favourable business environment by attracting capital, encouraging entrepreneurship. As a result, the municipality established supporting institutions like business zones, local development agencies and business incubators. There are 6 industrial zones on the territory of 30 ha out of which some are still in the phase of construction.

4.2 Municipality Bosansko Grahovo

Bosansko Grahovo is the municipality located at the border of BH with Croatia. In the period before the Civil War (1991-1995) the municipality counted 8.311 people, out of which working age population was employed with the 100 per cent rate. The active and successful firms were: Wood industry, Treset, shoe factory Borac, ball bearing production at Unis, highly equipped tilery... There were not enough workers to cover the needs of institutions, factories and industry. People from other municipalities were finding employment in Bosansko Grahovo. However, during the war, 98 per cent of infrastructure was destroyed and not renewed after. Today, the number of inhabitants is 75 per cent lower compared to the 1991 Census. The municipality has the lowest population density in whole BH (table 1). It is predominantly rural with very unfavourable age structure. Around 40 per cent of population are older than 65 years of age and only 5 per cent are younger than 18. Natural population increase is negative as well as migration balance which implies future negative trends in population structure. It is of great essence to develop the programs which would keep young population, offer them employment, better quality of life, social and cultural activities.

The municipality is abundant with natural resources which represent potential for the development of tourism like mountain Sator, three beautiful natural lakes, cave Ledenica...

The first problem related to natural resources is related to their management and utilisation. There is uncontrolled and illegal cutting of forest trees which also has a negative effect on water springs. This is caused because the jurisdiction upon natural resources is not on the level of municipality but on the level of Canton. It is necessary to develop a strategy based on natural resources, with special accent on the development of forestry, agriculture, especially animal husbandry. Natural landscape should not be neglected regarding the potential for tourism development. The tourism is not developed because there is no tourism-oriented infrastructure and adequate human capital. The potential lies in the development of mountain and hunting tourism and further on development of cycle tourism by cooperating with other municipalities. The tourism product should be branded as rural with different gastro offer and traditional products of households.

Related to built capital the main problem is lack of main services like the pharmacy, health centre, kindergarten, bank, high school, bakery, bus station and accommodation for guests. If in a need of a doctor the residents need to travel 30 km to the nearest town Drvar or even 110 km to the Cantonal hospital if they need a specialist. With the new governance, the health services were cancelled and transferred to Drvar municipality. The municipality is missing a Social Service Centre, and there are around 160 households without any kind of income or less than 200KM per household. One third of them receives social aid of 50KM a month.

The second problem related to built capital is the water supply. The people in this municipality don't have drinking water, and nobody concerns how they live under those conditions, how they transport water and what kind of access do elder people have when it comes to drinking water. The water seems to be luxury good in this municipality especially during dry seasons which start at May and end in November. This also can become even bigger problem if we consider the fact that there is no waste management and that the waste is removed every second or third month.

When it comes to social capital people consider themselves very passive, adapted to this unfavourable situation. Informal meetings and lack of joint action is limiting the change. The people are blaming local and cantonal government but are not doing anything to change it. There is lack of trust in the local government but also lack of power to influence it.

According to the official statistics in 2013 there were 70 registered business entities. However, the reality is completely different. Out of this number the active one are one small and one micro company. Others are bankrupt or without any information about them. The people that are employed are mainly working in public institutions like public administration, post, educational institution, police or small private stores. The average salary in the municipality is 986KM which is above the Canton (840KM) and Federation average (833KM). This could imply that the economic situation is not so bad, however this is the result of people being employed in public institutions where the salaries are above average. There are no business or industry zones and incubators.

5.   CONCLUSION

By deep analysis of the area, which is only partially presented in this paper, we can state that both areas are facing similar problems related to all capitals (assets) we evaluated. However, the degree of development is evidently different, and that is what is limiting, or making it harder to have integral and sustained progress recently in the future.

Both case studies are abundant with natural resources, especially forests, however jurisdiction, which is not on the local level is limiting effective management and utilization that would be beneficial for the municipalities first.

The main difference is visible related to built and institutional capital. The low performing municipality is lacking many of the public services which are creating unfavorable conditions for normal life. That can be one of the reasons for negative demographic trends. Likewise, absence of cultural capital and low social capital are only contributing to the poor conditions in the area that has unused potential. The causes could be found in inefficient local government, that is not working for the wellbeing of the community and that has limited power and skills to plan, implement and promote development.

The problems of both regions are not only the level of development of each capital, but very low level of capital accessibility and utilization to create or increase competitiveness of the municipalities and create opportunities for residents to improve their skills, knowledge, find employment, take joint actions and induce changes.

6.   ACKNOWLEDGEMENT

This research is partially funded by International Burch University as Internal Research Project under the title: ""Rural Development through Good Governance and Higher Capitals Utilization".

REFERENCES

Acquaah, M, Amoako-Gyampah, K, Gray, B and Nyathi, NQ 2014, Measuring and Valuing Social Capital: A Systematic Review. Network for Business Sustainability South Africa, viewed 16 October 2015, nbs.net/knowledge.

Agarwal Sheela, Rahman, S, Errington, A 2009, Measuring the determinants of relative economic performance of rural areas, Journal of Rural Studies, Vol. 25, No. 3, pp. 309-321

Becker, GS 1964 Human capital: A theoretical and empirical analysis with special reference to education, New York: Columbia University Press.

Bollman, R, Bryden, JM (Eds.) 1997, Rural employment. an international perspective, CAB International, Wallingford.

Braithwaite, K 2009, Building on what you have got: a guide to optimising assets, Carnegie UK Trust, Dunfermline, Scotland.

Brough, MK, Henderson, G, Foster, R, & Douglas, HA 2007, "Social Capital and Aboriginal and Torres Strait Islander Health - Problems and Possibilities", in Anderson, I, Baum, F & Bentley, M (eds.), Proceedings Social Determinants of Aboriginal Health Workshop, pp. 191-201, Adelaide.

Bryden, J & Munro, G 2000, New approaches to economic development in peripheral rural regions, Scottish Geographical Journal, Vol. 116, no. 2, pp. 111-124.

Bryden, J 2003, Rural Development Situation & Challenges in EU-25, Keynote Speech at EU Rural Development Conference, Salzburg, viewed 5 May 2015 http://ec.europa.eu/agriculture/events/salzburg/bryden.pdf

Bryden, J, Efstratoglou, S, Persson, L-O, Schrader, H, Atterton, J, Ceccato, V, Courtney, P, Efstratoglou, A, Hachmöller, G, Hart, K, Koch, B, Kouroussi, E, Masurek, L, Apostolos Papadopoulos, A, & Timm, A 2001, Dynamics of Rural Areas. Final Report.

Copus, AK, Courtney, P, Dax, T, Meredith, D, Noguera, J, Shucksmith, M, & Talbot, H 2011, Final Report. ESPON 2013 project EDORA (European Development Opportunities for Rural Areas), Project 2013/1/2, viewed 25 March 2015.

Crowe, JA 2006, Community Economic Development Strategies in Rural Washington: Toward a Synthesis of Natural and Social Capital, Rural Sociology, Vol. 71, No. 4, 573–596.

Dijkstra, L & Ruiz, V 2010, Refinement of the OECD regional typology: economic performance of remote rural regions DG Regio, European Commission.

Dower, M, 2013, "Rural development in the New Paradigm", in Kolczynski, M (ed.) New paradigm in action – on successful partnerships, Ministry of Regional Development, Warsaw, Poland.

European Commission (EC), 1997, Rural developments: situation and outlook. CAP, 2000 Working Document, Brussels.

Federal Development Planning Institution 2015, Socio-ekonomski pokazatelji po opcinama u Federacija Bosne i Herzegovine u 2014. godini.

Fey, Susan, Bregendahl Corry, and Flora Cornelia 2006, The measure of community capitals through research: a study conducted for the Claude Worthington Benedum Foundation by the North Central Regional Center for rural development, The Online Journal of Rural Research and Policy Vol. 1, No., pp. 1-28 viewed 22 July 2015 http://newprairiepress.org/cgi/viewcontent.cgi?article=1000&context=ojrrp

Flora, C, Flora, J, & Fey, S 2004, Rural Communities: Legacy and Change (2nd ed.), Boulder, CO: Westview Press.

Fritz, S M, Boren, AE, Trudeau, D, & Wheeler, DW 2007, Low resources in a high stakes game: Identifying viable rural community partners, Journal of Extension, Vol. 45, No. 4, viewed 5 July 2015, http://www.joe.org/joe/2007august/rb2.php

Geertz, C 1993, The interpretation of culture: Selected essays, Fontana Press, US

Goodland, R & Daly, H 1996, Environmental sustainability: Universal and non-negotiable, Ecological Applications, Vol. 6, No. 4, pp. 1002-1017

Kilkenny, M 1993, Rural vs. urban effects of terminating farm subsidies, American Journal of Agricultural Economics Vol. 75, no. 4, pp. 968- 980.

Kilkenny, M 1998, Transport costs and rural development, Journal of Regional Science, Vol. 38, no. 2, pp. 293-312.

Kilkenny, M 1999, Explicitly spatial rural-urban computable general equilibrium, American Journal of Agricultural Economics, Vol. 81, no. 3, pp. 647-652.

Krugman, P 1993, First nature, second nature, and metropolitan location. Journal of Regional Science, Vol. 33, no.2, pp. 129-144.

Krugman, P 1999, The role of geography in development. International Regional Science Review, Vol. 22, no. 2, pp. 142-161.

Lin, N 2001, Social capital. A theory of social structure and action, Cambridge: Cambridge University Press.

Matarasso, F 1999 Towards a Local Cultural Index. Measuring the Cultural Vitality of Communities. Comedia, Gloucestershire.

Ministry of Regional Development 2011, Effective instruments supporting territorial development, Strengthening urban dimension and local development. Issues paper produced for the Effective Instruments Conference, Warsaw, Poland http://www.mrr.gov.pl/konferencje/eic2011/eng/Documents/Issue_paper_EFTD_final.pdf

New paradigm in action on successful partnership, Ministry of Regional Development, Warsaw, 2013,

OECD 2006, The new rural paradigm: policies and governance, TDPC, Paris

OECD 2012, Promoting Growth in all Types of Regions, OECD Publishing, Paris

OECD, 1996. Territorial indicators of employment; focusing on rural development, OECD Publishing, Paris.

Porter, ME 1990 The competitive advantage of nations: Creating and sustaining superior performance, The Free Press, US

Prugh T, Costanza, R, Cumberland, J, Daly, HE, Goodland, R & Norgaard, RB 1999, Natural capital and human economic survival, 2nd edn, CRC Press - Lewis Publishers, Boca Raton, Fl.

Putnam, R 1995, Bowling Alone: America's Declining Social Capital, Journal of Democracy, Vol. 6, No. 1, pp. 65-78.

Putnam, R 2000, Bowling Alone: The Collapse and Revival of American Community, New York: Simon & Schuster.

Razvojna Agencija Zepce, 2011 Strategija razvoja opcine Zepce 2011-2018.

Reimer, B 2005, Rural and Urban: Differences and common ground in Hiller, HH, Urban Canada sociological Perspectives, Oxford University Press

Russo, MV 2003, The emergence of sustainable industries: building on natural capital, Strategic Management Journal, Vol. 24, no. 4, pp. 317-331

Skuras, D, Stathopoulou, Sophia 2000, Rural Entrepreneurship and regional development, Proceedings of 40th European Congress "European Monetary Union and Regional Policy", European regional science Association, Barcelona, Spain, viewed 21 April 2015, http://www-sre.wu-wien.ac.at/ersa/ersaconfs/ersa00/pdf-ersa/pdf/166.pdf

Terluin, IJ 2003, Differences in economic development in rural regions of advanced countries: an overview and critical analysis of theories, Journal of Rural Studies, Vol. 19, No. 3, pp. 327-344 viewed 18 April https://www.researchgate.net/publication/223697520_Differences_in_Economic_Development_in_Rural_Regions_of_Advanced_Countries_An_Overview_and_Critical_Analysis_of_Theories

Terluin, IJ, Post, JH (Eds.) 2000, Employment dynamics in rural Europe, CABI Publishing, Wallingford.

Torre, A 2014, New challenges for rural areas in a fast moving environment, European Planning Studies, Vol. 23, No. 4, pp. 641-649.

Tweten, Margaret, R 2008, Community Capitals: Examining the Socioeconomics of a Rural Community, Doctoral thesis, University of Dacota, USA

United Nations Trust Fund for Human Security 2015, Nacrt strategije razvoja opstine Bosansko Grahovo 2016-2020, (Strategy of Development of Municipality Bosansko Grahovo 2016-2020 - Draft Version);

Wakeford, R 2013, "Shaping rural futures – sustainable development for region-wide benefit" in Kolczynski, M (ed.) New paradigm in action – on successful partnerships, Ministry of Regional Development, Warsaw, Poland.

Westlund, H & Adam, F 2009, Social capital and economic performance: a meta-analysis of 65 studies, European Planning Studies, Vol. 18, No. 6, pp 893-919.

Whitener, LA, & Parker, T, 2007 Policy options for a changing rural America, Amber Waves, No. 5. Economic Research Service, US, Department of Agriculture, http://www.ers.usda.gov/AmberWaves/May07SpecialIssue/Features/Policy.htm

APPENDIX

FEDERATION OF BOSNIA AND HERZEGOVINA

Municipality	Employ. rate (%)	Unemploy. rate (%)	No. of pupils/1000	GDP per capita	Outmigration index	Development index	Rank 2014	change in ranking from 2009	Rural Type**	% of people in urban area	Canton**	Popul. density 2014	Proximity to large urban center
Centar	59,1	16	165	33.309	-13,3	235,1	1	0	PU	96,1	SAK	1795,1	
Čitluk	33,8	31,9	176	7.582	5	157,5	2	3	PR	18,2	HNK	102,5	Čitluk - Mostar, 22.5 - al
N.Sarajevo	31,6	27	116	20.211	-18,9	150,8	3	(-)1	PU	97,8	SAK	6949,7	
													Žepče - Zenica. 40.6
Žepče	14,7	52,2	140	2.210	35,2	147,9	4	0	PR	18,4	ZDK		112 km - about 40 mins
Neum	23,7	27,4	97	12.583	0,9	144,3	5	(-)2	I	65,2	HNK	22	
Ilidža	28	39,9	131	7.130	2,6	136,4	6	6	PU	95,1	SAK	501,3	
Tuzla	23,8	39,7	128	9.386	0,1	134,3	7	(-)1	I	66,9	TZK	409,7	
Stari Grad	23,5	39,6	123	17.263	-15,7	134,1	8	(-)1	PU	98,3	SAK	757	
Široki Brijeg	24,1	40	163	7.782	-2,6	132,4	9	(-)1	PR	21,6	ZHK	76,9	Široki Brijeg - Mostar, 2
Tešanj	20,7	43,8	141	4.234	11,2	132,1	10	(-)1	PR	12	ZDK	295,9	
Mostar	26,6	36,1	132	10.916	-11	129,2	11	0	I	57,7	HNK	96,3	
Posušje	19	41,6	204	5.339	-6,2	121,4	12	3	PR	30,9	ZHK	44,9	Posušje - Mostar, 50.9 k
Banovići	19,9	51,9	113	9.258	-2,4	119	13	(-)3	PR	28,6	TZK	126,7	Banovići - Tuzla, 148 km
Gračanica	16	53,4	124	3.588	11	118,2	14	0	PR	27,7	TZK	224,1	
Grude	19,7	37,2	145	5.532	-5,2	116,4	15	4	PR	24,7	ZHK	80,9	Grude - Mostar 42.38, le
Teočak	6	80,9	117	2.346	-21,1	49,3	65	0	PR	35,8		262,3	
Maglaj	15,6	58,7	127	3.688	-41,2	47,9	66	2	PR	25,8	ZDK	86,1	Maglaj - Zenica, 55 km,
Vareš	13,4	49,9	85	12.161	-55,5	47	67	(-)10	PR	32,6	ZDK	24,5	Vareš - Sarajevo, 49.4 kr
Jajce	12,1	58	136	4.990	-44	45,8	68	3	PR	26,3	SBK	90,7	Jajce - Banja Luka, 71.5
Odžak	14,4	51,3	114	4.548	-46,1	43,6	69	3	PR	43		134,4	Odžak - Tuzla, 83.8 km,
Donji vakuf	11,1	66	144	3.729	-43,4	40,1	70	(-)4	I	70,8	SBK	46,1	
Drvar	8,7	58,2	59	3.242	-32,6	40	71	(-)4	I	52,8	LVK	12,7	
Ključ	7,7	63,5	81	3.604	-36,5	36,1	72	(-)3	PR	28,9	USK	52,3	Ključ - Banja Luka, 67.4
Bosanski Petrova	16,2	50,6	118	5.012	-55,1	36,1	73	(-)3	PR	47,6	USK	11,3	Bosanski Petrovac - Bar
Domaljevac Šama	9,5	52,6	56	3.841	-51,7	19,3	74	1	I	78,8		117,5	
Foča (FBH)	12,7	62,3	75	10.147	-69,8	15,2	75	2		0	BPK	13,1	Ustikolina - Sarajevo, 87
Pale	10	59,4	72	3.189	-54,5	14,3	76	(-)2		0	BPK	12,1	Pale - Sarajevo, 41.8 km,
Glamoč	12,1	51,5	86	3.873	-64,8	10,3	77	(-)1	PR	48,8	LVK	3,9	Glamoč - Banja Luka, 12
Bosansko Grahov	17,4	46,9	41	8.597	-76	8,9	78	0	PR	28,3	LVK	4	Bosansko Grahovo - Ba
Dobretići	6,7	72,2	25	0	-86,9	(-)53.3	79	0		0	SBK	34,6	Dobretići - Zenica, 60,3

**TZK Tuzlanski Kanton
ZHK Zapadno Hercegovački
ZDK Zeničko Dobojski Kanton
HNK - Hercegovačko Neretvanski
SBK Srednje Bosanski
LVK Livanjski Kanton 10
USK Unsko Sanski
POK Posavski
BPK Bosansko Podrinjski
SAK Sarajevo Kanton

*Predominantly Urban U - above 85
Intermediate I - 50-85
Predominantly rural PR - lower than 50

Source: Statistika.ba; Federal Development Planning Institution 2015, Socio-ekonomski pokazatelji po opcinama u Federacija Bosne i Herzegovine u 2014. godini.